# SIN, FORGIVENESS, AND RECONCILIATION

## PREVIOUSLY PUBLISHED RECORDS OF BUILDING BRIDGES SEMINARS

*The Road Ahead: A Christian–Muslim Dialogue*, Michael Ipgrave, editor (London: Church House, 2002)

*Scriptures in Dialogue: Christians and Muslims Studying the Bible and the Qur'ān Together*, Michael Ipgrave, editor (London: Church House, 2004)

*Bearing the Word: Prophecy in Biblical and Qur'ānic Perspective*, Michael Ipgrave, editor (London: Church House, 2005)

*Building a Better Bridge: Muslims, Christians, and the Common Good*, Michael Ipgrave, editor (Washington, DC: Georgetown University Press, 2008)

*Justice and Rights: Christian and Muslim Perspectives*, Michael Ipgrave, editor (Washington, DC: Georgetown University Press, 2009)

*Humanity: Texts and Contexts: Christian and Muslim Perspectives*, Michael Ipgrave and David Marshall, editors (Washington, DC: Georgetown University Press, 2011)

*Communicating the Word: Revelation, Translation, and Interpretation in Christianity and Islam*, David Marshall, editor (Washington, DC: Georgetown University Press, 2011)

*Science and Religion: Christian and Muslim Perspectives*, David Marshall, editor (Washington, DC: Georgetown University Press, 2012)

*Tradition and Modernity: Christian and Muslim Perspectives*, David Marshall, editor (Washington, DC: Georgetown University Press, 2012)

*Prayer: Christian and Muslim Perspectives*, David Marshall and Lucinda Mosher, editors (Washington, DC: Georgetown University Press, 2013)

*Death, Resurrection, and Human Destiny: Christian and Muslim Perspectives*, David Marshall and Lucinda Mosher, editors (Washington, DC: Georgetown University Press, 2014)

*The Community of Believers: Christian and Muslim Perspectives*, Lucinda Mosher and David Marshall, editors (Washington, DC: Georgetown University Press, 2015)

# SIN, FORGIVENESS, AND RECONCILIATION

## CHRISTIAN AND MUSLIM PERSPECTIVES

*A Record of the Thirteenth Building Bridges Seminar*

Hosted by Georgetown University

Washington, District of Columbia & Warrenton, Virginia

April 27–30, 2014

**LUCINDA MOSHER and**
**DAVID MARSHALL, Editors**

GEORGETOWN UNIVERSITY PRESS
*Washington, DC*

Library of Congress Cataloging-in-Publication Data

Building Bridges Seminar (13th : 2014 : Washington, D.C.), author.

Sin, forgiveness, and reconciliation : Christian and Muslim perspectives : a record of the Thirteenth Building Bridges Seminar hosted by Georgetown University Washington, District of Columbia & Warrenton, Virginia April 27–30, 2014.
pages cm
Includes index.
ISBN 978-1-62616-284-6 (pbk. : alk. paper) — ISBN 978-1-62616-285-3 (ebook)
1. Christianity and other religions—Islam—Congresses. 2. Islam—Relations—Christianity—Congresses. 3. Sin—Christianity—Congresses. 4. Sin—Islam—Congresses. 5. Forgiveness—Religious aspects—Christianity—Congresses. 6. Forgiveness—Religious aspects—Islam—Congresses. 7. Reconciliation—Religious aspects—Christianity—Congresses. 8. Reconciliation—Religious aspects—Islam—Congresses. I. Mosher, Lucinda, editor. II. Marshall, David, 1963- editor. III. Title.
BP172.B834 2016
261.2'7—dc23
2015022043

∞ This book is printed on acid-free paper meeting the requirements of the American National Standard for Permanence in Paper for Printed Library Materials.

17 16 9 8 7 6 5 4 3 2 First printing

Printed in the United States of America

Cover design by N. Putens. Cover art © istockphoto.com/melissahelddesigns.

# CONTENTS

Participants ix
Introduction xi

## PART I: OVERVIEWS

**Sin, Forgiveness, and Reconciliation: A Christian Perspective** 3
*Veli-Matti Kärkkäinen*

**Sin, Forgiveness, and Reconciliation: A Muslim Perspective** 13
*Jonathan A. C. Brown*

## PART II: SIN

**Changing Places: Understanding Sin in Relation to a Graceful God** 23
*Christoph Schwöbel*

**The Concept of Sin in the Qurʾān in Light of the Story of Adam** 40
*Ayman Shabana*

**Scripture Dialogues on Sin** 66
Dialogue 1 66
*Romans 5:11–21* 66
*Genesis 3:1–24* 67
Dialogue 2 69
*Al-Aʿrāf (7):10–27* 69
Dialogue 3 70
*Romans 7:14–25* 70
*Al-Aʿrāf (7):177–79* 70
*Yūsuf (12):18* 71
*Yūsuf (12):53* 71

## PART III: FORGIVENESS

**Forgiveness and Redemption in Christian Understanding** 75
*Susan Eastman*

**Divine Forgiveness in Islamic Scripture and Thought** 83
*Mohammad Hassan Khalil*

**Scripture Dialogues on Forgiveness** 90
Dialogue 4 90
*Luke 15:11–32* 90
Dialogue 5 91
*Al-ʿAṣr (103):1–3* 91
*Al-Zumar (39):53–59* 91
*Al-Anʿām (6):128* 92
Dialogue 6 92
*Romans 8:1–4* 92
*Hūd (11):106–8* 92
*Al-Nabāʾ (78):21–30* 92
*Al-Aʿrāf (7):40–43* 93
Additional Qurʾān Passages 93
*Al-Anʿām (6):12* 93
*Al-Anʿām (6):54* 93
*Al-Aʿrāf (7):52* 94
*Al-Muʾminūn (23):109–18* 94

## PART IV: RECONCILIATION

**Reconciliation Between People: Christian Perspectives** 97
*Philip Sheldrake*

**Reconciliation and Peacemaking in the Qurʾān** 107
*Asma Afsaruddin*

**Scripture Dialogues on Reconciliation** 118
Dialogue 7 118
*Matthew 18:21–35* 118
Dialogue 8 119
*Āl ʿImrān (3):102–3* 119
*Al-Anfāl (8):61–63* 119
Dialogue 9 119
*Ephesians 2:11–22* 119
*Al-Ḥujurāt (49):9–13* 120
*Al-Mumtaḥina (60):7–9* 120

## PART V: REFLECTION

**Conversations in Virginia** 125
*Lucinda Mosher*

Index 139
About the Editors 145

# PARTICIPANTS

Professor Asma Afsaruddin, Indiana University, Bloomington, Indiana

Dr. Afifi al-Akiti, University of Oxford, UK

Dr. Amir Akrami, Eastern Mennonite University, Harrisonburg, Virginia

Professor Ahmet Alibašić, University of Sarajevo, Bosnia and Herzegovina

Professor Zainab Alwani, Howard University School of Divinity, Washington, DC

Professor Naumana Amjad, University of the Punjab, Pakistan

Professor Najib Awad, Hartford Seminary, Hartford, Connecticut

Professor Jonathan A. C. Brown, Georgetown University, Washington, DC

Professor Maria Dakake, George Mason University, Fairfax, Virginia

President John J. DeGioia, Georgetown University, Washington, DC

The Reverend Dr. Susan Eastman, Duke Divinity School, Durham, North Carolina

Dr. Brandon Gallaher, University of Exeter, UK

The Reverend Lucy Gardner, St Stephen's House, University of Oxford, UK

Professor Sidney Griffith, Catholic University of America, Washington, DC

Dr. Feras Hamza, University of Wollongong in Dubai

The Reverend Dr. Toby Howarth, National Inter Religious Affairs Adviser for the Church of England

Professor Mohsen Kadivar, Duke University, Durham, North Carolina

Professor Veli-Matti Kärkkäinen, Fuller Theological Seminary, Pasadena, California

Professor Mohammad Hassan Khalil, Michigan State University, East Lansing, Michigan

Professor Daniel Madigan, SJ, Georgetown University, Washington, DC

Professor Joel Marcus, Duke University Divinity School, Durham, North Carolina

The Reverend Dr. David Marshall, Duke University Divinity School, Durham, North Carolina

Dr. Jane McAuliffe, Distinguished Visiting Scholar, Library of Congress, Washington, DC

Shaykh Ibrahim Mogra, Muslim Council of Britain

Dr. Esther Mombo, St Paul's University, Limuru, Kenya

Dr. Lucinda Mosher, Hartford Seminary, Hartford, Connecticut

Professor Feryal Salem, Hartford Seminary, Hartford, Connecticut

Abdallah Schleifer, Senior Fellow, Royal Aal al Bayt Institute for Islamic Thought, Jordan

Professor Christoph Schwöbel, University of Tübingen, Germany

Professor Ayman Shabana, Georgetown University School of Foreign Service in Qatar

Professor Philip Sheldrake, Westcott House, University of Cambridge, UK

Professor Janet Soskice, University of Cambridge, UK

# INTRODUCTION

**LAUNCHED IN 2002** as an initiative of the office of the Archbishop of Canterbury and since 2013 under the stewardship of Georgetown University, the Building Bridges Seminar—a gathering of scholar-practitioners of Islam and Christianity—convenes annually for deep study of selected texts pertaining to an overarching theme, such as scripture, prophethood, science and religion, or prayer. Care is taken to have a near-equal number of Muslims and Christians—emerging scholars alongside seasoned experts. While the Christian delegation has always been heavily Anglican and Catholic, Orthodox and Protestant scholars have been included regularly—as was the case for the 2014 seminar. Similarly, while the Muslim delegation is always predominantly Sunnī, Shi'a scholars have always been included. The seminars have always included a substantial number of women scholars. The circle of dialogue is diverse in other ways as well. Since the seminar's founding, the venue for discussion has alternated between Christian-majority and Muslim-majority contexts.

This book digests the proceedings of the thirteenth annual Building Bridges seminar, convened in and near Washington, DC, April 27–29, 2014. Since the twelfth annual Building Bridges seminar had examined Christian and Muslim perspectives on death, resurrection, and human destiny, it seemed a logical next step to explore questions of sin, forgiveness, and reconciliation. Georgetown University president John J. DeGioia was present as host and participant. As he had in 2013, Daniel Madigan, SJ, Jeanette W. and Otto J. Ruesch Family Associate Professor in Georgetown's Department of Theology, assumed the role of convenor.

Georgetown University's Riggs Library provided an elegant setting for a pair of public lectures surveying the seminar's overall theme from an Islamic and a Christian perspective. The seminar then transferred to the seclusion of the Airlie Center in Warrenton, Virginia, for three days of closed meetings featuring a pair of short lectures on the day's topic followed by three ninety-minute sessions of dialogical study of preassigned scripture texts. The organization of the present volume reflects this pattern.

Thus, part 1, "Overviews," provides the complete text of the opening lectures. In "Sin, Forgiveness, and Reconciliation: A Christian Perspective," Veli-Matti Kärkkäinen (Fuller Theological Seminary) discusses notions of sin and the Fall in Christian tradition, contrasting Orthodox with Western (Catholic, Anglican, and Protestant) interpretations. He stresses Christianity's distinctive linking of forgiveness with reconciliation in incarnational atonement theology. He then explores the relationship between Christian notions of divine forgiveness of human beings and forgiveness among human persons and communities. In turn, this leads him to discuss the relationship between theological understandings of forgiveness and reconciliation and the hard work of peace building and conflict resolution. Jonathan A. C. Brown (Georgetown University) uses a current news report as a point of departure in offering his perspective on "Human Sin, Divine Forgiveness, and Human Reconciliation in Islam." These terms, Brown explains, are linked to each other on both vertical and horizontal planes. Thus he explores Islamic understandings of human sin against God; human sin against fellow humans; God's forgiveness of human beings; and human beings' forgiveness of each other as a reflection of God's mercy.

Parts 2, 3, and 4 each feature two essays on one of the core concepts identified in the seminar theme. During the seminar itself, these lectures served to introduce to the gathered scholars the scripture passages that would be taken up in small-group discussions during the remainder of the day. Those texts have been provided in full, following their introductory essay.

Part 2, "Sin," opens with essays by Christoph Schwöbel and Ayman Shabana. In "Changing Places: Understanding Sin in Relation to a Graceful God," Schwöbel argues that "the Christian theological exploration of sin is based on the sign system of Christian faith"—that is, "on the biblical witnesses, ordered in the doctrinal traditions and exercised in the practices of worship." He surveys ways found in the Bible to identify sin and describe liberation from sin. He gives particular attention to Romans 5 as a Pauline commentary on the Genesis account of the temptation of Adam and Eve, to the inevitability of sin, and to the history of Christian doctrinal debates regarding sin. In "The Concept of Sin in the Qur'ān in Light of the Story of Adam," Shabana clarifies Qur'ānic vocabulary associated with sin and lays out the Qur'ān's master narrative on sin. He surveys the treatment of the story of Adam in *tafsīr* literature, using al-Ṭabarī and al-Rāzī as exemplars of report-based and opinion-based exegesis and *Tafsīr al-Manār* of Muḥammad ʿAbduh and Rashīd Riḍā as an example of Qur'ānic exegesis in the early twentieth-century context. He then describes the role of the Qur'ānic Adam narrative in debates concerning such issues as the nature of Iblīs and his relationship to the angels, the status of prophets vis-à-vis angels, the infallibility of prophets, human freedom and destiny, the status of sinners, and the impact of sin on belief.

Part 3, "Forgiveness," features Susan Eastman's essay "Forgiveness and Redemption in Christian Understanding" and Mohammad Hassan Khalil's "Divine Forgiveness in Islamic Scripture and Thought." Eastman explains two "views of the human need for God and God's way of salvation in Christian teaching and, indeed, in the New Testament itself" that both interlock and are in tension with each other: the view, on the one hand, that "all human beings are guilty of sinful actions for which they need divine forgiveness," and the notion, on the other hand, that "all humanity is in bondage to 'Sin' as a supra-individual, and perhaps supra-human, power from which we need deliverance and liberation." She begins by comparing the behavior of the father in Luke 15:11–32 (the parable of the prodigal son) with the view of parental responsibility laid out by the Jewish sage Ben Sira (early second century BCE) in Sirach 33:20–24, drawing out four lessons about forgiveness. She then turns to examples—such as Jesus's healing of a paralytic (Mark 2:1–12; Matt. 9:2–8) and Jesus's crucifixion itself—of the "countercultural power of forgiveness." She then contextualizes Romans 8:1–4 as a passage within a Pauline epistle chapter focused on redemption, both as "deliverance from *condemnation for sin*," and "also freedom from the *compulsion to sin*." She concludes by summarizing "themes uniting Luke's account of forgiveness and Paul's account of redemption."

Given the Qur'ān's testimony to God's forgiving nature, Khalil explains the Qur'ānic criterion for successful attainment of divine mercy. He surveys Qur'ān verses and ḥadīths regarding God's prerogative to forgive sins and the relationship of divine forgiveness to human repentance. He then discusses the range of Islamic views on what constitutes *shirk* and whether even the damned might eventually enjoy divine redemption.

In part 4, "Reconciliation," essays by Philip Sheldrake and Asma Afsaruddin address Christian perspectives on reconciliation between people and Muslim perspectives on reconciliation and peacemaking in the Qur'ān. Given today's "radically plural and often violently divided global culture," Sheldrake sees engagement with inclusivity and diversity, otherness and alienation as critical spiritual issues. Before introducing Matthew 18:21–35 and Ephesians 2:11–22, Sheldrake clarifies the meaning of *reconciliation* as a key Christian theological term. He explains reconciliation not only as God's free and loving action but also as a continuing human (not only Christian) vocation that involves changing places with "the other." Reconciliation has, therefore, a close relationship with hospitality. Arguing that "the vocation of proclaiming human reconciliation is not incidental to Christian life but lies at its very heart," he introduces the Rule of St.

Benedict and the Eucharist as "Christian resources for what might be called a spirituality of reconciliation."

In her essay, Afsaruddin asserts that, from a Qur'ānic perspective, the human heart—understood as "the basic cognitive and emotive center of the human system"—is "the most important site for bringing about genuine individual change followed by social change." When the heart is made more receptive to God's will, it also becomes more able to cultivate fraternity and to overcome enmity. Her survey of exegeses of several Qur'ān verses provides insight into the method the Qur'ān offers for "effecting reconciliation and fostering peaceful relations among people."

Concluding this volume, part 5, "Reflection," offers the essay "Conversations in Virginia," in which Lucinda Mosher, assistant academic director of the Building Bridges Seminar, shares anecdotes and insights from the 2014 plenary and small-group discussions, providing the reader with a sense of the tone and level of engagement among the participants.

Readers of *Sin, Forgiveness, and Reconciliation* may desire suggestions for further engagement with the themes on which it focuses. For perspectives on Christian theology, see *Christ and Reconciliation: A Constructive Christian Theology for the Pluralistic World* by Veli-Matti Kärkkäinen (Wm. B. Eerdmans Publishing, 2013); *The Theology of Reconciliation*, edited by Colin Gunton (Bloomsbury T&T Clark, 2003); or *Sin: The Early History of an Idea* by Paula Fredriksen (Princeton University Press, 2012). For understandings of Islamic points of view, see *Between Heaven and Hell: Islam, Salvation, and the Fate of Others*, edited by Mohammad Hassan Khalil (Oxford University Press, 2013); and "Reconciliation in Islamic Theology" by Mahmut Aydin, in *Journal of Ecumenical Studies* (39, no. 1–2 [Winter–Spring 2002]: 141–50).

Throughout this volume, when not indicated otherwise in the text or endnotes, the translations of the Qur'ān either are from M. A. S. Haleem, *The Qur'an: A New Translation* (Oxford: Oxford University Press, 2004), or are the author's own translation. Unless otherwise indicated in the text or notes, Bible selections are from the New Revised Standard Version of the Bible, copyright 1989 by the Division of Christian Education of the National Council of the Churches of Christ in the USA. Used by permission. All rights reserved.

Deep appreciation is extended to Georgetown University president John J. DeGioia for his ongoing support of the Building Bridges Seminar. Georgetown University's Berkley Center—particularly, its director, Thomas Banchoff—provides a base of operations and online presence for the seminar and has made the publication of this book possible. As for previous seminars, David Marshall and Daniel Madigan took leadership in setting the theme, organizing the circle of scholars, and choosing the texts to be studied. Many people played a role in the success of the 2014 gathering, particularly Samuel Wagner, coordinator for Catholic and Jesuit Initiatives in the Office of the President, who provided logistical support. The staff members of the Airlie Center were gracious hosts. Finally, gratitude is extended to Richard Brown and the staff of Georgetown University Press.

# PART I

▲ ▲ ▲

# Overviews

# Sin, Forgiveness, and Reconciliation

## *A Christian Perspective*

VELI-MATTI KÄRKKÄINEN

**LET ME BEGIN** with three observations as an orientation to sin and the Fall in Christian theology.[1] First, while all Abrahamic traditions believe that there is something wrong with us and the world because of sin, these sister faiths do not envision sin's origin and results in the same way. Whereas Christian theological tradition speaks of "original sin" (and even "total depravity"), Islamic tradition rejects such an interpretation of the Adam and Eve story. Second, even the Jewish and Christian interpretations of the same scriptural materials yield widely differing theologies of sin. In Jewish theology the "fallen" state of humanity is understood as being driven by either evil or good inclinations, and unlike in the New Testament–based Christian exegesis, Adam plays virtually no role.[2] Third, against common intuitions, within the Christian tradition there are widely differing ways of conceiving the results of the Fall and sinfulness. To oversimplify a complex issue, we can describe the two main Christian traditions in the following manner:

1. The less "negative" interpretation is that of the Eastern Orthodox Church, in which the Fall narrative is depicted as a "stumbling" of yet-immature children (Adam and Eve). While of course a sad experience, the Fall did not bring about original sin and certainly did not bring about divine judgment. Rather, judgment comes only as a result of wrong choices and acts. The effects of the Fall are understood more as a wound inflicted in our nature.
2. The more "negative" interpretation is present in the traditions of the Christian West, which include Roman Catholic, Anglican, and Protestant churches. Following St. Augustine's theology, they speak of original sin as the result of Adam's disobedience; this sinfulness, which results in divine judgment, is "inherited" from generation to generation. That said, there is a divergence within

the Christian West between the two main families. As will be discussed in the following, Augustinian thought develops somewhat differently in the Roman Catholic, Anglican, and Protestant traditions.

An important corollary issue behind theologies of sin and the Fall is the question of the freedom of the will. Whereas in the Christian East freedom of the will was not negated by Adam's disobedience, the Christian West, following Augustine, denies the power of choice apart from divine restorative grace (except for freedom to choose wrongly!). Before the Fall the human being was capable of not sinning, but that capacity was totally lost thereafter. Protestant and Anglican churches continued affirming this Augustinian denial of freedom of the will (apart from grace), whereas in Roman Catholicism, mainly owing to St. Thomas Aquinas, a somewhat less negative account of the will developed.[3] Recall Luther's work *The Bondage of the Will* (1525) in rebuttal of the Catholic humanist Erasmus of Rotterdam's *The Freedom of the Will* (1524).[4] Anglican and Protestant traditions also derived from Augustine the idea of "double predestination," that is, from all eternity God has decided to save some and lead others to eternal damnation. The Eastern Church vehemently rejects that theory, and Roman Catholicism does not teach it (despite all its indebtedness to Augustine).[5]

As mentioned, the figure of Adam (and Eve) plays a critical role in Christian theology of sin not only because of the Genesis 3 narrative but especially because of St. Paul's discussion in Romans 5. It is widely agreed in contemporary Christian theology that even if in Pauline theology the universality of sin is traced back to Adam (Rom. 5:12), there is not yet an idea of sin "as a fated universal legacy that proliferates generation after generation like a congenital disease."[6] And although Paul teaches the universal occurrence of death (Rom. 5:12, an idea familiar also to Jewish tradition), he does not speak of inheritance of sin in any technical sense. Eastern Orthodox theology followed that tradition in understanding the example and sin of Adam as representing the whole race instead of linking this notion to the idea of inheritance of sin. It is highly significant that patristic theology (theology of the church fathers) for centuries did not have a developed doctrine of sin (other than a deep intuition of the fallen and sinful nature of humanity). Only with St. Augustine at the turn of the fifth century was a technical doctrine of original sin worked out.[7] The basic idea is that when Adam sinned, we participated in it. This interpretation was supported by the faulty Vulgate translation of Romans 5:12, which translated the Greek *eph ho* as "in whom," that is, when Adam transgressed, we, the human race, participated in his sin, and we inherit this fallen nature from our parents.[8] We are guilty and condemned as a result.[9]

In the Christian East the human was regarded as mortal even before the Fall and hence death per se cannot be punishment for the Fall. Human nature is intact even after the Fall and is good by virtue of existing as the image of God, and free will is not destroyed by the Fall. In this interpretation, we do not inherit sin but rather its consequences, particularly corruption and mortality. In other words, the East followed the Hebrew mind-set in which even the concept of original sin is not a standard term. While the universality of sin is affirmed, in Eastern theology, as mentioned, it is often described in terms of woundedness or sickness.

Having now described the differences of interpretations of sin and the Fall in Christian tradition, I should add the following remarks lest I be misunderstood. Notwithstanding many disagreements among the Christian traditions concerning the hermeneutics of "fall" and "original sin," there is no denying the simple fact that (quoting the late Reformed theologian Paul Jewett) while "no religious vision has ever esteemed humankind more highly than the Christian vision," no other tradition has also "judged it more severely."[10] Similarly, the great ethicist-theologian of the past generation R. Niebuhr reminds us, "A theology which fails to come to grips with this tragic factor of sin is heretical both from the standpoint of the gospel and in terms of its blindness to obvious facts of human experience in every realm and on every level of moral goodness."[11] In sum, all Christian traditions believe that something is wrong with us and the world to the point that unless God in his grace and mercy stoops down to our level and forgives us, we are without hope. To that gracious divine offering of forgiveness and reconciliation we turn next. But before that, an important additional note concerning the huge challenges brought about by modernity and the Enlightenment.

As a result of the dramatic changes in our worldview thanks to scientific breakthroughs, including the acceptance among mainline Christian traditions of evolution and the account of the emergence of the cosmos in light of contemporary physical sciences, Christian theology of sin has to revise some key assumptions—without in any way softening the fact of our sinfulness. The traditional assumptions in need of revision include the historicity of Adam and Eve, the "innocence of the Paradise," the linking of sin with our physical death, and the "timing" of the Fall. Very briefly put, this means that "universal" sinfulness can be affirmed in the context of evolutionary theory's view of the slow emergence of humanity. Rather than being historical, the Genesis 3 narrative of Adam and Eve is understood as a myth that nevertheless contains an important religious truth; as a result, the idea of innocence of Paradise is neither directly taught in the Bible nor reasonable in light of evolutionary emergence. Finally, physical death cannot be made the function of the Fall. Death and decay has been in place for billions and billions of years before the emergence of humanity and simply characterizes the finite life of the creature. These revisions have already been made among Christian churches (apart from most traditional and conservative communities)—as they were in mainline Jewish traditions. I would be interested to hear from Muslim participants their sense of how contemporary Muslim thought has dealt with these same challenges.

## Divine Forgiveness and Reconciliation

All Abrahamic traditions anchor the possibility of forgiveness and reconciliation in God; indeed, "in forgiveness, the grace of God is ultimately at work."[12] Using their own terminology, both Judeo-Christian and Islamic scriptures extol the merciful and gracious nature of God. Even the different diagnoses of the sinfulness of humanity do not make these foundational theological statements obsolete. The distinctively Christian teaching is the linking of forgiveness and reconciliation in the atonement theology: God became human in Jesus Christ (incarnation), suffered and died for our sins, and in his glorious resurrection gained victory over judgment and death. This kind of atonement theology is of course not part of either Jewish or Islamic theology and is strongly rejected by both.[13] As it does with regard to the doctrine of sin, Christian tradition speaks of atonement in more than one voice, although all Christian churches affirm a Christological (and Trinitarian) basis. For the first millennium or so, the main way of speaking of atonement involved so-called *Christus Victor* (Christ the Champion) metaphors, which focus on incarnation, resurrection, and *theosis* (deification). Rather than speaking of atonement mainly in terms of guilt and judgment, which became the focus in the Christian West beginning in the medieval period, this "recapitulation" theory of atonement (St. Irenaeus) primarily emphasizes overcoming corruption and mortality by virtue of participation in the divine life. Many other metaphors of atonement emerged at the beginning of the second millennium, including Satisfaction (Anselm of Canterbury), Moral Example (Peter Abelard), Penal Substitution (Protestant Reformers), and so forth. They are complementary ways of embracing the multifaceted and rich salvific benefits of Christ's work on our behalf.[14]

While divine forgiveness is the foundation and source, Christian tradition—in keeping with the common teaching of all Abrahamic traditions[15]—also emphasizes the importance of forgiveness and reconciliation among human beings and communities. This section focuses on divine forgiveness and the next section on forgiveness among men and women.[16]

The topic of forgiveness is treated widely in the biblical tradition; just recall its centrality in the ministry of Jesus of Nazareth and of his followers.[17] Forgiveness is also mentioned in the ecumenical Nicene-Constantinopolitan Creed (381 CE) in connection with the Holy Spirit and the church. Indeed, in the life of the church, forgiveness is also integrally linked with sacramental life, particularly water baptism and the Eucharist.

The Christian notion of divine forgiveness is of course deeply indebted to Jewish scriptures.[18] Although turning to God (repentance) is required (2 Kings 17:13–14; Jer. 3:11–14)—meaning that refusal to do so may lead to withdrawal of forgiveness (Isa. 22:14; Jer. 5:1–9)—the later prophets also emphasize that what really matters is the right attitude rather than mechanical following of cultic practices (Amos 5:21–25; Isa. 1:11–17; Hosea 6:6). In the New Testament Gospels, the main words used for forgiveness are *aphiemi* (let go, cancel, remit, leave) and *aphesis* (release, pardon, cancellation). That the term *forgiveness* appears rarely in the rest of the New Testament does not mean that the idea is therefore marginal. On the contrary, St. Paul and others refer to the same concept using a host of other metaphors, such as justification, reconciliation, redemption, and the like. And even in the Gospels, the idea of forgiveness may be present even if the word is missing, as in the parable of the prodigal son in Luke's Gospel (15:11–32).

If forgiveness is based on divine mercy, are there any conditions for its reception? What is striking about Jesus's ministry is the seeming generosity of forgiveness. Not only did he pronounce forgiveness to "sinners" (a technical term for those outside the covenant), but he even included them in table fellowship (the highest sign of inclusion in that culture). On the other hand, there is no denying the link between repentance and forgiveness, both in Jesus's own ministry (Mark 1:15) and in keeping with that of his predecessor, John the Baptist (Mark 1:4). Furthermore, the same mandate is given by the risen Lord to the disciples (Luke 24:46–47), and the early church carries on with this tradition (Acts 2:38, 5:31, 8:22, 26:18). What are we to make of the relationship, if any, between repentance and forgiveness? While Christian tradition does not speak unanimously,[19] it seems to me that according to the mainstream New Testament witness, neither repentance nor any other human preparation should be made a prerequisite: "God unilaterally makes forgiveness possible by offering forgiveness 'while we were yet sinners' (Rom. 5:8)."[20] That said, it also seems to me that while divine forgiveness is unconditional, based as it is on God's mercy and atonement gained by the salvific work of Christ, its reception calls for repentance. In other words, repentance, rather than a precondition, is a necessary result or consequence of divine forgiveness. In other words, the refusal to repent means saying no to the divine offering of forgiveness. This principle of unconditional forgiveness should also guide our understanding of forgiveness between humans. We are called to forgive our enemies and violators simply because God has forgiven us. To that topic we turn in the last section of this presentation.

## Forgiveness and Reconciliation among Human Persons and Communities

While God's forgiveness is the basis and source, all Abrahamic traditions also emphasize the necessity of extending forgiveness to the neighbor. Like the Holy Qur'ān, the First Testament—the shared scripture between Jews and Christians—contains numbers of well-known historical narratives of forgiveness, such as Joseph forgiving his brothers (Gen. 45:1–15, 50:15–20); Moses, the people of Israel (Exod. 32:11–14, 30–33; Num. 12:11–13); and David, his son Absalom (2 Sam. 14:21, 33). Jesus spoke often of the need to extend forgiveness not only to our neighbors but even to those who violate us.

Having received divine forgiveness, an unconditional gift, we humans are called to imitate that act of hospitality. In forgiving, humans mediate the gift of forgiveness they have received themselves. Miroslav Volf locates forgiving in the context of two opposing movements, namely, "Embrace or Exclusion." *Exclusion* may happen in many ways, including elimination (as in ethnic cleansing), assimilation (when acceptance is based on the demand to be like us), domination, and abandonment. *Embrace*, in contrast, is based on "the outstretched arms of Christ on the cross for the 'godless,'" the welcoming by the father of the prodigal son. This "will to embrace" includes both opening to the other and drawing into intimate touch and "opening the arms," letting go, that is, making space for the otherness of the other.[21]

God has reconciled the world to Himself (2 Cor. 5:17–20) and empowers humans to spread that reconciling influence at the personal and communal levels. The one who forgives refuses to pay back the violator. Forgiveness is hence a costly effort; it calls for self-sacrifice. It often hurts. In this sense it can be said that the victim undergoes suffering in two moments: first in the act of being violated against and then in the willingness to suffer in offering the gift of forgiveness.

Psychologists tell us that forgiveness is good for the soul; it has positive effects on the one who forgives. While that may be true, in Christian faith that goal is secondary. Forgiveness is not done primarily for the sake of one's own well-being but because of neighborly love to which followers of Christ are called in the imitation of their heavenly Father, who loves without any conditions and without any distinctions. It is done for the sake of others. Indeed, it is also done for the benefit of the violator. Forgiveness helps also the willing violator to begin the process of reconciliation and his own healing. Offering forgiveness not only helps the violator to deal with the past, it also points to the future opportunity. It is an act of trust.

A long tradition of philosophical and theological reflection on forgiveness has linked it with resentment.[22] In this view, forgiveness primarily means a process of overcoming resentment, the feeling of anger caused by having been the object of wrongdoing. A version of this view is that forgiveness is supposed to free the wronged person from all forms of negative feelings, even disappointment. While certainly a good thing, getting beyond resentment has little to do with the theology of forgiveness as presented by Jesus. Jesus invites us not only to "turn the other cheek" (which of course entails a real experience of being wronged) and embrace the offender in forgiveness but also to expose the wrong act for the sake of justice and so that the wrongdoer might find reconciliation in accepting guilt and receiving forgiveness. It has to be said definitively that forgiveness—neither divine nor human—does not trump justice and righteousness. Restoration cannot happen without the wrongdoing being exposed and judged.

Hence, folk psychology's advice "forgive and forget" is a profoundly mistaken idea. The one who is concerned about both justice and reconciliation must learn how to "remember rightly." Forgiveness does not mean instant—or often even long-term—erasure of the victim's memory. Recalling rightly is required for the sake of exposing and judging all wrongdoings. Jesus said, "If your brother sins against you, go and tell him his fault, between you and him alone. If he listens to you, you have gained your brother" (Matt. 18:15). But we have to understand that this condemnation of a wrong act is not based on the principle of retributive justice; neither is it about vengeance. It is about reconciling justice.

Remembering rightly is also needed for the sake of healing both the victim and the wrongdoer. Mere forgetting can be nothing more than a way of repressing negative memories, leaving the victim with enmity and hatred. Rather than forgetting or suppressing the act of wrongdoing, recalling it helps the violator to ask for and receive forgiveness and be reconciled with the victim, with one's self, and with God. The violator who accepts forgiveness also accepts the condemnation. By refusing to receive forgiveness, the offender lets others know that he or she did nothing wrong. That blocks the way to reconciliation with other people and God.

Christian theology of atonement and forgiveness condemns violence and wrongdoings. It also helps stop them and saves us from the cycle of revenge. Maximus the Confessor put it succinctly: "The death of Christ on the cross is a judgment of judgment."[23] Violence may happen both at personal and communal (even societal) levels. The common task for all Abrahamic traditions is to collaborate in stopping violence. The Rwandan theologian Celestin Musekura, whose country has experienced a colossal massacre and much violence, has called on churches and religious communities to become communities of forgiveness and reconciliation:

> Forgiveness as a virtue is learned not in an isolated, self-excluded life but rather in a community of faith where members of the community experience

> the reality of sin and brokenness together. Today's stories of genocide, mass murder, racism, tribalism, religious wars, terrorism, and church conflicts indicate not only the fragility of our commitment to life in community of friendship and embrace but also how difficult it is for individuals to unlearn the habits of sin of exclusion by domination, elimination, abandonment, and assimilation, and to the extreme by genocide.[24]

This reconciliatory work should also lead us to the work of peace building and conflict resolution. Recently the World Council of Churches's International Ecumenical Peace Convention made this programmatic statement: "We understand peace and peacemaking as an indispensable part of our common faith. Peace is inextricably related to the love, justice and freedom that God has granted to all human beings through Christ and the work of the Holy Spirit as a gift and vocation. It constitutes a pattern of life that reflects human participation in God's love for the world."[25]

## Notes

1 This section is based on my detailed discussion of sin and the Fall in Christianity and four other faith traditions (Judaism, Islam, Hinduism, and Buddhism) in chap. 15 of *Creation and Humanity*, vol. 3 of my *Constructive Christian Theology for the Pluralistic World* (Grand Rapids, MI: Eerdmans, 2015). Consequently, the documentation herein is kept at a minimum. I am grateful for Dr. David Marshall for feedback and encouragement during the drafting of this presentation. I have incorporated some of his comments and insights into the presentation (although, of course, all inaccuracies or mistakes are my own).

2 The obvious reason for the Jewish conclusion is that in the Tanakh Adam virtually disappears after the opening pages. One has to wait until 2 Esd. (7:48) to know that Adam's fall has universal effects (but that each individual may also win over sin, 7:57).

3 Behind the Thomist (and Anselmian) continuation and modification of the Augustinian doctrine is the "two-story" anthropology based on a nature–grace dialectic. Whereas intellect and will belong to the realm of nature, the supernatural gift of "original righteousness" (as well as supernatural "virtues" of faith, hope, and love) belong to that of grace. As a result, the latter can be removed (as happened as a result of the Fall) without destroying the "natural" endowments (even though they too were hampered severely because of sin). Clearly, at the center of Thomas's theology is not the Fall but rather the supernatural destiny of human nature.

4 Interesting in this regard is the fact that one of the first works of St. Augustine (before his battle with Pelagianism) was *On the Free Choice of the Will*.

5 A detailed discussion of freedom of will in relation to the issue of salvation is in chapter 9 of my *Spirit and Salvation*, vol. 4 of *A Constructive Christian Theology for*

*the Pluralistic World* (Grand Rapids, MI: Eerdmans, 2015). Furthermore, a discussion of human freedom (vis-à-vis determinism) in relation to contemporary sciences, particularly brain study, and philosophy of mind appears in chapter 13 of my *Creation and Humanity*. Both of these discussions also engage the previously mentioned four living faiths and their interpretations.

6 Wolfhart Pannenberg, *Anthropology in Theological Perspective*, trans. Matthew J. O'Connell (Philadelphia: Westminster Press, 1985), 121.

7 Among many relevant writings, the most important in this regard is Augustine's *Treatise on the Merits and Forgiveness of Sins, and on the Baptism of Infants*. Augustine is of course not the only advocate of the traditional Western Church's view (just recall his mentor Ambrosius's influence). But he is the most prolific and authoritative witness. Recall that the Antiochene theologian Theodore of Mopsuestia's *Against the Defenders of Original Sin*—a telling title—forcefully argued that only human nature can be inherited, not sin.

8 An asset in the hereditary interpretation of sin came from the Traducianist view of the origin of soul (that is, at moment of conception the human being to be born receives her "nature" from both parents rather than directly from the Creator, as in the "creationist" view).

9 *Augsburg Confession* #2 (a key Lutheran confessional document) puts it this way: "since the Fall of Adam all humans who are propagated according to nature are born in sin," and this "vice of origin is truly sin, which even now damns and brings eternal death on those who are not born again through Baptism and Holy Spirit."

10 Paul Jewett, *Who We Are: Our Dignity as Human; A Neo-Evangelical Theology*, with Marguerite Shuster (Grand Rapids, MI: Eerdmans, 1996), 57.

11 Reinhold Niebuhr, *Christianity and Power Politics* (New York: Charles Scribner's Sons, 1940), 17–18.

12 L. G. Jones, "Crafting Communities of Forgiveness," *Interpretation* 54 (2000): 122 [121–34].

13 Generally speaking, the main difference between Christian and Islamic traditions in this respect is that whereas in the former, forgiveness "costs" God (and, hence, requires a sacrifice or satisfaction or similar), in Islam God just forgives, without any sacrifice. For a detailed comparison of Christian, Jewish, and Islamic interpretations of "salvation" (including also Buddhist and Hindu traditions), see my *Christ and Reconciliation*, vol. 1 of *A Constructive Christian Theology for the Pluralistic World* (Grand Rapids, MI: Eerdmans, 2014), chap. 15 (and also chap. 10, focused on the role of Christ).

14 For a detailed discussion and constructive theology, see part 2 of my *Christ and Reconciliation*.

15 A detailed study of forgiveness (and repentance as well as conversion) in Christian and other Abrahamic traditions (including also Asiatic faiths) can be found in my *Spirit and Salvation*, chap. 10. This and the following section are based on that discussion, and therefore documentation is kept at a minimum.

16 Currently, forgiveness is also a topic of great interest in behavioral sciences (particularly in psychology), sociology, philosophy, and so forth. Those studies will not be involved here (but are engaged in chap. 10 of my *Spirit and Salvation*).

17 Let it suffice to list key passages in one Gospel: Matt. 6:12, 14–15, 9:2, 5–6, 12:31–32, 18:21–23, 35, 26:28.The command to preach repentance and forgiveness of sins was given by the resurrected Christ to his followers (Luke 24:47), and the early church practiced it regularly (2:38).

18 The main Hebrew terms for forgiveness in the OT are *nāsā* (whose main meaning is "to carry" and "release"; Gen. 18:26; Ps. 25:18; 32:1, 5; Isa. 33:24), *sālah* (used only in reference to God's forgiveness; Lev. 4:20, 5:6; Num. 14:19; Isa. 55:7), and *kipper* ("to make atonement," only used of divine forgiveness, as in Isa. 22:14).

19 Beginning in the early centuries of the church, repentance also came to be linked with the more or less technically defined rite (and process) of penitence. In the course of history, particularly in the Western church, the influence of a Roman legally oriented concept of justice (particularly in Tertullian) led to the tight linking of forgiveness with repentance and penitence. Particularly important was the Roman demand of satisfaction as the prerequisite for forgiving (an idea St. Anselm later made a leading theme). A related important development was the emerging distinction between sins forgiven at baptism and those committed after baptism (which sometimes led to the postponement of baptism until one's deathbed). By the fifth century an elaborate "Order of Penitents" was put in place, and later the rite of penance became one of the sacraments.

20 Jesse Couenhoven, "Forgiveness and Restoration: A Theological Exploration," *Journal of Religion* 90, no. 2 (2010): 165. And recall that the first words from the cross as narrated by Luke (23:34) were "Father, forgive them; for they know not what they do."

21 Miroslav Volf, *Exclusion and Embrace: A Theological Exploration of Identity, Otherness, and Reconciliation* (Nashville, TN: Abingdon, 1996), 29, 72–77, 141.

22 A formative influence came from the eighteenth-century Bishop Butler's famous series of sermons on forgiveness at Rolls Chapel.

23 Maximus the Confessor, *Questions to Thallassius*, 43.

24 Celestin Musekura, "An Assessment of Contemporary Models of Forgiveness" (PhD diss., Dallas Theological Seminary, 2007), 156–57.

25 "Glory to God and Peace on Earth: The Message of the International Ecumenical Peace Convocation," May 17–25, 2011, Kingston, Jamaica. For important theological contributions to communal reconciliation, peace building, and conflict resolution, see the numerous writings of the Catholic Robert J. Schreiter, such as *Reconciliation: Mission and Ministry in a Changing Social Order* (Maryknoll, NY: Orbis, 1992); and *The Ministry of Reconciliation: Spirituality and Strategies* (Maryknoll, NY: Orbis, 1998).

# Sin, Forgiveness, and Reconciliation

## *A Muslim Perspective*

JONATHAN A. C. BROWN

**IN THE SPRING OF 2014,** in the northern Iranian city of Nur, a murderer was taken to the gallows. With the rope around his neck, blindfolded and grimacing with fear, he heard a woman's voice cry out. It was the mother of his victim announcing at the last moment that she forgave the killer for his crime. Tears streaming down his face, the condemned man was released from the noose. His mother rushed to embrace the mother of his victim, and both sobbed—one over a son lost, one over a son regained.[1]

The man had been convicted of the crime of murder. Had he in fact committed that sin? It is possible that the witnesses who testified in court had lied, leading to a false conviction. It is also possible that the judges had not noted how, somehow in the heat of an argument, the man had acted in self-defense. Only God knows. As Muslim scholars—in their capacity as judges—have insisted for centuries in a veteran legal maxim, "We have been commanded to rule on what is evident, and God knows the hearts." All that the Sharīʿa court in Nur knew was that evidence and procedure had determined that, in this world at least, the man had taken the life of another. And the victim's family had rights. As declared by the Qurʾān, "Retaliatory punishment has been ordained for you in the matter of murder" (al-Māʾida [5]:45 et al.).

Although it was the right of the victim's family members to see the killer executed, the Qurʾān also allowed them to accept monetary compensation or even to forgive the killer entirely. This had been the course taught by the Prophet Muḥammad, who had never ruled on a case of murder without urging the victim's kin to forgo the punishment and forgive the murderer.[2] There is perhaps no better way for me to convey the possibility of human reconciliation here on Earth than the image of the two Iranian mothers embracing. The victim's mother had decided to forgive the killer after her son appeared to her in a dream, telling her that he was in paradise as a martyr, all his sins forgiven. What fate awaited his killer, spared for now, in the afterlife? The Qur'ān warns that "whosoever slays a believer intentionally, his reward is Hellfire forever" (al-Nisā' [4]:93).[3] Humans can forgive each other, but God forgives whom He wills.

Only a few Muslim countries are still ruled by God's law, the Sharī'a, but this episode in Iran is illustrative of how the Islamic tradition has conceived of the three daunting themes of human sin, divine forgiveness, and human reconciliation. In those moments on the gallows, we can glimpse the vertical and horizontal axes linking them. Man sins against God, offending upward an all-powerful, invincible Creator. And man sins against man, injuring an all-too-vulnerable fellow human being, a human being whom God has granted the right to repair. God forgives, sending His mercy down upon sinners. God forgives, and perhaps His mercy spreads among the people. Humans forgive and begin to reconcile, in a sense reflecting God's mercy.

Let us look at each of these elements in turn. At the base of the vertical axis of sin and forgiveness connecting man and God lies our own human nature. All too familiar to us, revelation tells us more of our human proclivity to sin, our vile baseness in iniquity, and our glory in righteousness. Mankind is hasty, the Qur'ān says, ungrateful, quick to despair, too liable to follow the herd around them rather than the right guidance of God's messengers. As God describes in the Qur'ān, "Indeed We created man in the best of forms, and then We reduced him to the lowest of the low. Except those who believe and do good deeds" (al-Tīn [95]:4–6). When the children of Adam "assail the obstacle," the loftier but more difficult of "the two paths" (al-Balad [90]:10–11) laid out by God before them, by acknowledging their Lord and doing right, they rise higher than angels, who praise and worship God constantly but could never do other than that. But when the children of Adam deny their Lord and sin, making their own desires their gods, "then they are no more than beasts, nay farther astray than them" (al-Furqān [25]:44). Unlike animals, these reprobates chose their torpid path, while animals do no more than follow their nature and thus praise God constantly along with the trees and heavenly bodies.

At the top of the vertical axis of sin and divine forgiveness is God's response to our actions, that of "the best of judges" (al-Tīn [95]:8), who "does not wrong any of His servants" (al-Anfāl [8]:51). Those who denied Him in this life and did evil "will be engulfed in what they were want to do," and the fires and torments of Hell will be an otherworldly manifestation of their vile conduct and misguided beliefs.[4] For those who believe and do good deeds, however, their good will be magnified. God promises in the Qur'ān that He "will ward off from them the worst of their deeds and will reward them for the best that they used to do" (al-Zumar [39]:35).

Thus, alongside God's justice at the top of the vertical axis is his infinite mercy toward His creation. In response to Moses's pleas for aid in dealing with the recalcitrant Israelites before Mt. Sinai, God says that He will grant felicity to those who believe and do good deeds. "My punishment, I strike with it those whom I wish. And my mercy encompasses all things" (al-Aʿrāf [7]:156).[5] The Qurʾān instructs Muḥammad, "Say: O my servants who have trespassed against themselves, do not despair of the mercy of God, for indeed God forgives all sins, indeed He is most forgiving and merciful" (al-Zumar [39]:53).[6] God warns that He forgives all sins except associating partners with Him. But even this limit is qualified, concluded Muslim scholars, since those who repent as well as those pagans or non-Muslims who never knew Islam or never learned of its true teachings are forgiven for their idolatry and misguidance.[7] God instructs Muḥammad to tell those new converts to Islam who repented their former ways that their sins are forgiven, for "Your Lord has prescribed mercy upon Himself" (al-Anʿām [6]:54).[8] Because, as God decreed before the creation of the universe, "My mercy overwhelms my anger."[9] He can forgive even the worst sinners. "O child of Adam," Muḥammad tells us that God decreed, "even if your sins reached as high as the ladders of the sky, and then you asked my forgiveness, I would forgive you."[10]

Because of the enormity of God's mercy, and because the scope of His cosmic justice so far exceeds our ken, the result is that we cannot know who will enter heaven and who will not. Muḥammad once told of two Jews in ancient times, one of whom was pious and admirable and the other of whom was an open sinner. The righteous man would tell his friend to amend his ways, to which the sinful man would reply, "Leave me be, me and my Lord." Finally, the pious man told his friend, "God will never forgive you or allow you to enter the Garden of Heaven." When both their souls were taken upon death, God said to the pious man, "Did you know Me or control My power?" God bestowed His ultimate clemency and paradise upon the iniquitous man and condemned the otherwise pious man to hell for the sin of arrogance.[11] We cannot know how God will judge any mortal, and it is sheer hubris to delimit His mercy.

This brings us to the horizontal axis of sin, namely, our temporal judgment of sins in the earthly world. Here we are torn between two undeniable truths we have already mentioned. On the one hand, God has made clear to us that certain beliefs and actions displease Him: denying His blessings and bounty, believing that others besides Him can help or harm us, committing slander, lying, dishonoring one's parents, stealing, becoming intoxicated, and backbiting. These are all sins. As the Qurʾān states, "God forbids shameful deeds, and what is wrong and overweening" (al-Naḥl [16]:90). Muslims of all sects have agreed that it is a Muslim's duty to enjoin right and forbid wrong, and some of these sins require the temporal authorities to punish those who commit them here on Earth. Such was the case with the murderer in Iran. Whoever takes a life unjustly has committed so tremendous a sin in God's eyes that, as the Qur'ān states, "it is as if he has killed all of humankind" (al-Mā'ida [5]:32). Along the horizontal axis, it is left to those empowered with judgment in state and society to ensure that the family of the slain receives justice (al-Isrā' [17]:32–33).

On the other hand, however, we cannot be sure of any necessary link between the horizontal and vertical, between the enormity of a sin or false belief and the fate of the sinner in the afterlife. The labels of believer or unbeliever, Christian, Muslim, or Jew are thus only markers of "legal faith (*īmān shar'ī*)," or the confessional categories into which people fit to determine their legal relationships to each other, their rights and obligations. They have no necessary link to "faith of conscience (*īmān fitrī*)," or an individual's faith in God, which ultimately determines his salvific destiny. A Muslim is buried in a Muslim graveyard, a Christian in a Christian one. A Christian man cannot marry a Muslim woman according to the Sharī'a. Muslims can be prosecuted for drinking and intoxication or for selling wine, while a Christian cannot. Of course, this does not mean that Muslims make no assertions about the rightness or wrongness of beliefs. "Whoever desires other than Islam as religion, it will not be accepted from him, and he will be among the losers in the world to come" (Āl 'Imrān [3]:85).[12] But merely belonging to the formal legal and social category of those following the correct religion means nothing for an individual's fate. Someone who is legally a Muslim may suffer horrendously in hellfire for his personal atheism, gross misconduct, or perfidious acts. A God-fearing, righteous Christian may attain salvation long before him on the basis of his belief in God and good deeds. According to Muslim (Sunni and Imami Shī'i) doctrine, all monotheists will one day enter paradise after the torments of hell have burned their sins away.[13] Thus, as Muslim scholars often cite in their didactic poems, "Do not declare that any one person will go to Hell, nor to Heaven, if you follow Muḥammad's precedent."[14]

The clarity of what constitutes crimes and the rules that God has revealed for adjudicating human conduct, taken along with the unknowable perfection of God's justice and the magnitude of His mercy, constrain our treatment of sin in this world to the realm of formalism. Along the horizontal access of human reconciliation, this formalism is accompanied by an emphasis on the value of reconciliation above and independent of which party is right and which party is wrong. The Qur'ān reads:

> If two parties among the believers battle one another, then reconcile between them. But if one of them transgresses beyond bounds against the other, then fight you all against the one that transgresses until it complies with the com-

> mand of God. But if it then complies, make peace between them with justice and equity, for God loves those who are fair. The believers are brethren, so reconcile peacefully between your two brothers. And fear God, that you may receive His mercy. (al-Ḥujurāt [49]:9–10)

The vanity of conflict between the Children of Adam, even (and perhaps particularly) when one group feels assured of God's favor, is clear also when the Qur'ān instructs Muslims on dealing with non-Muslims. Muḥammad is told in the Qur'ān how to approach the enemy tribes fighting the Muslims: "But if the enemy inclines towards peace, then incline towards peace also, and trust in God, for indeed He is the all-hearing, omniscient" (al-Anfāl [8]:61). While writing about Jihād, one sixteenth-century Egyptian jurist recalled a story of King David. While building the Temple, everything David constructed would crumble. God spoke to him, saying, "My house will not be erected by the hands of one who has shed blood." David pleaded that he had only fought wars in God's name. "Indeed," God replied, "but were those who died not also my servants?"

Acts like that of the Iranian mother granting clemency to her son's killer are close to pure mercy. But in other cases of humans wronging each other, the essential role of mercy in human reconciliation is clear. A party must be willing to offer the amorphous gift of mercy rather than insisting formally on its rights. This was a central theme in the procedure of Sharī'a courts (and also in the less glamorous, mundane affairs of arbitration here in the United States). Throughout Islamic civilization, judges followed the dictum that "Peaceful reconciliation is best." Even if one party had clearly wronged another, it was always deemed best if both parties could compromise and meet on middle ground. This would ultimately reduce the possibility of further conflict.[15]

Eventually the horizontal axis of humans extending mercy to one another (whether in the course of reconciliation or not) angles upward once again to the divine. The Prophet Muḥammad's teachings emphasize that human acts of mercy are reflections of the apotheosis of mercy in the godhead. But they are not disinterested acts, as reflecting God's attributes is an act of worship and thus has its rewards. "Those who are merciful," the Prophet once said, "the Most Merciful God has mercy upon them. Be merciful in this world, and He that is in the Heavens will have mercy upon you."[16] In another saying Muḥammad teaches that "he who is not merciful will be granted no mercy."[17] Even in the case of the Iranian mother pardoning her son's killer, the Qur'ān emphasizes that the benefit accrued is ultimately mutual. The family of the slain can demand reciprocation, but as the Qur'ān continues, "whosoever forgoes it out of charity, this is an expiation of his/her own wrongs" (al-Mā'ida [5]:45).[18] Mercy and reconciliation thus become acts of worship directed upward along the axis to God accompanied by the promise of mercy sent downward in return.

In addressing these complicated and vast topics, I have almost certainly neglected much that should be said and may well have said something incorrect. Rather than closing with a conclusion, I think I'll leave you with at least one fully opened can of worms. Submerged gleefully in the baroque scholasticism of the nineteenth century, a leading Muslim jurist noted the question of whether someone who has committed a crime such as fornication or murder can excuse himself by citing divine preordination—"God willed this for me." One can cite predestination to avoid blame, the scholar says (in Sunni Islam humans have only the illusion of free will), but not to avoid the mandated punishment or liability. This scholar cites as his evidence a saying of the Prophet that caused great controversy in the classical Islamic period, when Muslim scholars debated hotly over the question of free will versus predestination. Adam sinned in the Garden of Eden and fell from it, the Qur'ān tells us, but God forgave mankind that original sin (Ṭā Hā [20]:122–24). The Prophet told of the souls of Adam and Moses meeting in heaven and of Moses confronting Adam over his having cost all mankind a blissful life in the Garden. "How could you, O Moses, whom God has purified as a prophet and given the Torah, blame me for an act that God had ordained for me long before creation?" "And so Adam trumped Moses," Muḥammad concluded.[19]

## Notes

I wrote this from what I see as a Muslim perspective, not with the intention of excluding or offending others but rather in the hope of honest communication.

1 Saeed Kamali Dehghan, "Iranian Killer's Execution Halted at Last Minute by Victim's Parents," *Guardian*, April 16, 2014, http://www.theguardian.com/world/2014/apr/16/iran-parents-halt-killer-execution.

2 Sunan Abī Dāwūd: kitāb al-diyāt, bāb al-imām ya'muru bi'l-'afw fī al-dam.

3 Wa man yaqtul mu'minan muta'ammidan fa-jazā'uhu jahannamu khālidan fīhā.

4 Jalāl al-Dīn Muḥammad bin As'ad al-Dawānī, *Ḥaqīqat al-insān wa'l-rūḥ al-jawwāl fī al-'ālamīn*, ed. Muḥammad Zāhid al-Kawtharī (Cairo: al-Maktaba al-Azhariyya, 2006), 5.

5 'adhābī uṣību bihi man ashā'u wa raḥmatī wasi'at kulla shay'in.

6 qul yā 'ibādī alladhīna astrafū 'alā anfusihim lā taqnaṭū min raḥmat Allāh, inna Allāh yaghfiru al-dhunūb jamī'an innahu huwa al-ghafūr al-raḥīm.

7 This is well established, since the verse is specified by Qur'ān 39:53. See Ibn Taymiyya, *Majmū'at al-fatāwā*, 11:104; al-Albānī, *Fatāwā*, 350.

8 kataba rabbukum 'alā nafsihi al-raḥma.

9 raḥmatī taghlibu ghaḍabī; Ṣaḥīḥ al-Bukhārī: kitāb al-tawhīd, bāb qawlihi ta'ālā wa yuḥadhdhirukum Allāhu nafsahu.

10 Jāmiʿ al-Tirmidhī: kitāb al-daʿwāt, ḥadith # 3885; also Forty Hadith of Nawawi.

11 Sunan Abī Dāwūd: kitāb al-ādāb, bāb al-nahy ʿan al-baghy; al-Baghawī, *Sharḥ al-sunna*, ed. Shuʿayb al-Arnāʾūṭ (Damascus: al-Maktab al-Islāmī, 1983), 14:385.

12 There can be another conference on this!

13 Jāmiʿ al-Tirmidhī: kitāb al-ṭibb, bab ma jāʾa fī-man qatala nafsahu bi-ṣumm aw ghayrihi.

14 Wa lā taḥkumanna ʿalā aḥadin biʾl-janna / wa lā biʾl-nār in aradta al-sunna.

15 Wael Hallaq, *Sharia* (Cambridge: Cambridge University Press, 2009), 164–65.

16 Sunan Abī Dāwūd: kitāb al-adab, bāb al-raḥma.

17 Ṣaḥīḥ al-Bukhārī: kitāb al-adab, bāb raḥmat al-walad wa taqbīlihi.

18 Here it is interesting to note that the word used for forgoing the punishment is the same word used for giving voluntary charity (*taṣaddaqa*).

19 Burhān al-Bayjūrī, *Ḥāshiyat al-Bayjūrī ʿalā Jawharat al-tawḥīd*, ed. ʿAlī Jumʿa (Cairo: Dār al-Salām, 2006), 188; *Ṣaḥīḥ Muslim*: *kitāb al-qadr, bāb ḥijāj Ādam Mūsā.*

# PART II

# Sin

# Changing Places

## *Understanding Sin in Relation to a Graceful God*

CHRISTOPH SCHWÖBEL

**IN MOST WESTERN COUNTRIES**, which have been shaped by the cultural influences of Christianity, the word *sin* is in everyday discourse no longer understood in a religious sense as an offense against God or as a distortion of the relationship of humans to God. Moralistic uses of the word ("the sinful greed of the bankers"), trivializing references to sin ("the seven deadly diet sins"), or the invocation of sin to create a sultry atmosphere of erotic titillation prevail. The most significant aspect of our cultural situation is the interpretation of what was formerly seen as sin and its consequences as a pathological deviation that should be therapeutically dealt with. Sin as a state that formerly could be overcome only by God's grace has for many today become a question of human self-repair aided by therapeutic techniques. While Christian theologians often lament the loss or the distortions of a religious understanding of sin—a complaint that is by no means new, since Kierkegaard in his *Introduction to Christianity* (1850) already lamented the "abolition of sin"—it is interesting to see that secular scholars, sociologists as well as philosophers, find the notion of sin not only deeply fascinating but also irreplaceable for the diagnosis of the human condition and its self-interpretation.[1]

In contrast to the moralistic, trivializing, hedonistic, or therapeutic transformations of what was formerly understood as sin, all world religions, if they are in one way or another religions of salvation or redemption, persistently maintain a dissonance between what we are and what we are meant to be, a contradiction between the factual state of humans and their true destiny. This can be explained in various ways: as the consequences of a primordial evil deed; as the bondage of humans to a state of deception and delusion; or by the fact that humans are from the beginning divided beings, since both good and evil deities contributed their "gifts" to the creation of humans. The way in which reparation for evil actions, the acquittal of the agent, the liberation from a state of deception, and the overcoming of the intrinsic self-contradiction of humans is achieved is always relative to the center of meaning of a religion and bound into a system of worship, rituals, ethics, and belief. In our religiously pluralist settings, the religions keep a sense of sin awake insofar as they see the factual existence of humans challenged by deeper problems than moral failure or pathological deviations that are amenable to therapeutic correction. Interreligious conversation is therefore a way of exploring the dialectic between human self-assertion and self-loss in a way that goes beyond the superficialities of human self-interpretation by engaging with the sign systems of religious practice and experience.

The Christian theological exploration of sin is based on the sign system of Christian faith—as it is based on the biblical witnesses, ordered in the doctrinal traditions, and exercised in the practices of worship. Since revelation is understood as a process of sign giving that discloses the true state of humans in their relationship to God, this exploration carries with it specific truth claims. While this engagement with the disclosure of truth unites the religious traditions, the specific truth claims are often incompatible, which creates the need for clarifying conversations between the religious traditions.[2]

## Patterns for Discerning Sin

In the New Testament we find various ways for identifying sin and describing the liberation from sin. They are all based on the way sin is identified and expressed in the Old Testament. The most significant roots are *cht'*, "missing one's aim"; *'awôn*, summarizing the evil deed, guilt, and its consequences; and *pæsha*, denoting an (intentional) breach of a contractual obligation.[3] The Psalms in particular illustrate the rich dynamic of confessing one's sins, of asking for God's forgiveness, and of giving thanks for receiving pardon and thus being restored to the right place in the relationship to God and in the community. The Hebrew scriptures underline in various ways that sin can in no way be reduced to the understanding of a transgression of a divine commandment. In all its different forms, sin must be understood as a violation of the relationship that God intends for God's human creatures and in which humans find the fulfilment of their destiny. This violation of the relationship to God is in most places seen as a phenomenon that begins with the disorientation of the human heart and its desires and finds expression in external attitudes, dispositions, and actions.

When we turn to the New Testament, we find that the traditional ways of understanding sin are presupposed and continued.[4] In Jesus's message and actions, there does not seem to be any contradiction of what his contemporaries see as being sinful, thus qualifying people as sinners. The term *sinners*, as in the frequent combination of "tax-gatherers and sinners" (e.g., Mark 2:15–16; Luke 7:34, 15:1; Matt. 11:19), denotes all those who are seen to act consistently against the will of God in various ways and who are therefore excluded by the normative religious consensus of society, regardless of whether they are seen as morally suspect, ritually unclean, or doctrinally heterodox. Jesus's ministry is not concerned with redefining sin but is devoted to inviting those who are commonly regarded as sinners to his table fellowship and so—this is the claim implicit in his actions—reintegrate them into communion with God. This involves a dramatic reinterpretation of who sinners are. If we follow the two parables in Luke 15:1–10, sinners should be seen as the ones who were lost and who have now been found again. Their being found is interpreted by Jesus as their repentance, and so there will be joy in heaven about everyone who was lost and is now found. Repentance is redefined not by human acts of turning away from sin but by turning to Jesus, or rather by accepting his acceptance of sinners. Jesus's hospitality is thus implicitly understood as reception into the hospitality of God, and this enables and obligates sinners to turn away from sin.

It is this decisive shift in Jesus's ministry that underlies the new emphases in the understanding of sin in the various theological conceptions of the New Testament. The main models for understanding sin and liberation from sin (as debt and the cancellation of debt; as pollution and the cleansing of pollution; as sickness and healing) all emphasize the encounter with Jesus's word, work, and person as the turning point from the old state of sin to the new state of being forgiven. This Christological refocusing of the understanding of sin is perhaps most drastically expressed in John's Gospel and the Johannine tradition. Sin is understood as the failure to believe in Jesus as Son and revealer of God (cf. John 8:24). By faith in Jesus, the will of God is fulfilled, and so faith becomes the new logical complement, the theological opposite, of sin. In 1 John 5:18 we can even read: "We know that those who are born of God do not sin, but the one who was born of God protects them and the evil one does not touch them." Here an ethical understanding of sin is clearly transcended. What seems to be presupposed is the bold statement in John's Gospel that Jesus "takes away the sin of the world" (John 1:29) so that those who are in him and abide in him cannot be touched by sin (1 John 3:6–9).

## Paul: The Universality of Adam's Sin

Paul's understanding of sin is different from John's. His starting point, however, is a similar Christological refocusing of the framework of talking about sin. The universality of salvation for all who have faith in the gospel of Christ (Rom. 1:16–17) is correlated with the drastic statement of the anthropological universality of sin (cf. Rom. 3:9–18). This negative universality claim is intended to complement the promissory universality claim that all who have faith in Christ are now at peace with God (Rom. 5:1). To support this radical vision against the view attributed to the Jews, that belonging to the community of circumcision and keeping the law leads to salvation, Paul has to displace the significance of the law in the scheme of salvation. There is no difference between Jews and Gentiles, "since all have sinned and fall short of the glory of God" (Rom. 3:23). Adam's sin is introduced because it is both a transgression of an explicit commandment of God, and at the same time the fate in which all humans are included even before the law was given through Moses. Just as "the righteousness of God through faith in Jesus Christ" (Rom. 3:22) radically relativizes the difference between Jews and Gentiles—everybody can believe!—so reference to Adam's sin also has the point of relativizing this distinction. In this sense Adam is the "type of the one who was to come" (Rom. 5:14). The analogy works from Christ to Adam, from the universality of God's righteousness through faith to the universality of sin and condemnation in Adam. The evidence for this is that the generations between Adam and Moses have died, and "death is the wages of sin" (Rom. 6:23), although they have not transgressed a particular law of God and therefore their sin "is not reckoned" (Rom. 5:13)—that is, it cannot be accounted for as a violation of a particular law of God. Paul contrasts the transgression of Adam, its character, its effects, and its rule, first with the free gift of righteousness of God, which is then described in active terms as the act of one (Christ; Rom. 5:18), but this act again has the character of obedience (to God's will of righteousness). Although the formal logic is the analogy between one act and its consequences for many, the difference in content is that Adam's act is rebellion, a truly autonomous human act, whereas Christ's obedience is the exercise of God's will. What is in this way contrasted is the fate following the act of disobedience, death and the dominion of death, and the fulfilment of the human destiny, justification and eternal life. At this point the displacement of the law is complete. Faith in God's righteousness in Christ gives what the law promises: eternal life in communion with God. What then is the function of the law? It is simply that where more laws are given, more laws can be broken and have to be accounted for (Rom. 5:20), but this only shows that "grace abounded all the more" (Rom. 5:20), because the measure of grace is not the sinfulness of human acts of transgression but the abundance of God's righteousness.

## Looking Back at the Garden of Eden

One can read Paul's reflections on the universality of sin in the Adam–Christ typology of Romans 5 almost as a commentary on Genesis 3, which has served in Christian interpretation as the foundational story of the understanding of sin and "original sin." Although the technical terms for sin are not mentioned here,[5] the story has long been interpreted as the etiological narrative about the origin of sin and the fallen state of humanity. We can see that Paul refers back to Genesis 3 both to explain the misery of the human condition under the fate of sin and to present Christ as the fulfilment of God's original plan for God's human creatures in creation. The narrative is so rich in its exploration of the human being as being-in-relation that we can only highlight a number of its features:

1. Upon a canonical reading, we have to presuppose what is said about the place and mandate of humans in the order of creation in chapters 1 and 2, the priestly and the non-priestly account of creation. Humans, man and woman, are created in the image of God, they receive God's blessing and mandate to procreate and act as created representatives of the Creator in creation (Gen. 1:27–28). By this blessing and mandate humans are promised a future, a history in conversation with God. Humans are created as communicative beings who receive their guidance by God's address and are thus made responsible to God. Only God's images can sin! Only those to whom God turns in addressing them can turn away by neglecting or contradicting God's address.

2. Temptation occurs through another creature (the "serpent"), an element of the natural order, not a kind of antidivine supernatural power. It takes the form of questioning God's word.

3. The prohibition to eat from the tree in the middle of the garden is part of a great permission ("you may freely eat of every tree in the garden . . ." [Gen. 2:16]). It serves as a boundary condition, marking the existence of humans as one that is dependent on the guidance of the divine word and pointing to the intrinsic finitude of created being. The prohibition marks the difference between the Creator and God's created image and so discloses the character of their relationship. Humans have been granted finite, created freedom that is dependent on the communicative disclosure of the divine will.

4. The serpent offers a different promise, a different gospel ("You will not die" [Gen. 3:4]), and also offers insight into God's knowledge ("God knows . . ." [Gen 3:5]). The content of the promise of the serpent is as follows: "You will be like God, knowing good and evil." In the logic of the story, the offer of equality with God contrasts sharply with creation in the image of God because that consists in the destiny of living as the created image of divine freedom in finite freedom.[6] The promise of the serpent is different. The serpent invites humans to usurp the place of God in creation, by knowing good and evil as God knows them, by defining good and evil creatively through their sovereign will. Whereas God's human image knows good and evil through God's word in permission and prohibition, as promise and law, the existence of being like God implies defining

the standard of goodness independently of God the Creator, and so—automatically—against God the Creator. Knowing goodness independently of the Creator means grasping the status of the Creator in the relational order of creation.

5. To be a creature means to be a creature with desires. Having desires is an implication of the finite relational state of humans who find fulfilment in relation to other beings. The desires can be directed toward finding fulfilment in God, or they can be expressions of a finite being, desiring to compensate for its limitations by possessing other beings. Eve finds the fruit desirous to the senses and to the intellect. The goodness of God's creation (Gen. 2:9: "the LORD God made to grow every tree that is pleasant to the sight and good for food") becomes ambivalent once it is desired in the misdirected search for independent knowledge. The tree is to be desired "to make one wise" (Gen. 3:6). Indeed, the whole story of the Fall can be read as a conflict between two kinds of wisdom, one for which "the fear of the LORD is the beginning of wisdom" (Prov. 1:7, 9:10; Ps. 111:10), the exemplar of creaturely wisdom, and the other for which wisdom serves to be godlike.

6. In giving her husband the fruit to eat, Eve shares the temptation and the misdirected desire with Adam. Temptation is contagious.

7. The effect of giving in to temptation is the comprehensive *dislocation* of human beings in all the relationships in which they exist.[7] The first is the relationship to themselves. The promise of the serpent becomes true, the first humans acquire another knowledge, but it is one in which they perceive their nakedness as being shameful. They try to cover themselves. The violation of the relationship to the Creator always involves a distortion in the self-relation of the creature. The good gift of the Creator, the bodily nature of creatures, becomes tainted by ambivalence.

8. As the story goes on, it is shown how the distortion spreads into all relationships in which humans exist. God, the giver of everything creatures have, becomes a threat for the fallen creatures. They try to hide from God and do not want to be addressed (cf. Gen. 3:8–10). The sinner wants God to be silent. God, however, continues to maintain the communicative relationship with the fallen creature and so maintains also the human creatures' status as being responsible before God. "Where are you?" As an address to the creature in hiding, it is almost a disclosure of the dislocation of humans. When the man responds, he points to the distortion in his self-relation of which he has become aware: his shameful nakedness.

9. Called to account for what he has done, Adam—in order to avoid being held responsible—employs the greatest gift that God's images have been given: their responsibility as the capacity to respond to God. Adam shifts the blame to Eve and indirectly implicates God: "The woman whom you gave to be with me,

she gave me of the fruit from the tree . . ." (Gen. 3:12). The disruption in the relationship to God spreads to the relationship between humans. Ironically, this is also the first instance when the theodicy question is raised: How can God be justified for giving Adam a companion who then leads him into temptation? The good gifts of the Creator are presented as perverted by the fallen creature.

10. When it is the woman's turn to be questioned, she shifts the blame to the nonhuman creation: "The serpent tricked me" (Gen. 3:13).

11. When God delivers judgment, only the serpent is directly cursed. The following promise on the woman's offspring has often been interpreted as the "first gospel," pointing forward to Christ: "he will strike your head and you will strike his heel" (Gen. 3:15). The other sentences have as their content the preservation of the gifts and promises of createdness under the conditions of the Fall. The promise for humankind to have a future is upheld but connected with the pains of childbearing and birth (cf. Gen. 3:16). The companionship of the sexes continues but in the entanglement of desire for one another and rule over one another. The position of humans as God's representatives and stewards in creation is maintained but connected with strenuous labor (Gen. 3:17) until humans return to the ground from which they are taken. The common point of these sentences is that createdness is preserved under the conditions of being fallen. God's care even extends to the distortion of the self-relation of humans by clothing them with something more permanent than fig leaves (Gen. 3:21).

12. The first humans are expelled from the Garden of Eden, and historical time begins. The expulsion also serves the purpose of preventing the fallen creatures' eating from the tree of life and thereby living forever. What appears as a hard judgment is, in fact, a blessing. It means that the conditions of fallenness are not eternal, they are finite and they will end. Humans will not forever be dislocated in the relational order of creation; they are destined for being relocated.

Interpreted in this way, it seems clear that this etiological narrative is a sustained theological reflection on the features of the human condition that are part of the experience of every age. By telling the story of how these conditions of existence came about, the permanent characteristics of human relational existence are illumined and connected to the root of all evil: the desire to be more than human in grasping at the status of God the Creator.

## The Inevitability of Sin and Its Overcoming

When we now turn back to Paul, we can see what he saw as the upshot of the paradigmatic narrative of the Fall in Genesis 3. It is the permanent conflict between the flesh and the spirit, the interior side of the dislocation of humans in the order of location. Paul describes it here as being sold to sin as a slaveholder to whom humans are compelled to surrender their freedom. The law, that is, doing the will of God, belongs to the enlivening power of the spirit; the flesh characterizes the bondage of humans to sin. This is depicted as inevitable. Just as there cannot be any embodied existence without the flesh, so humans are bound to sin, inevitably. This introduces a permanent state of dividedness into human life that obscures human self-understanding. It is indeed a dramatic conflict in which human life is involved, doing what one does not want to do, knowing that the law is good but nevertheless not being able to follow what is known to be good (cf. Rom. 7:14–17). The contradiction permeates the whole human being, wanting with the mind what is good and life-giving but not being able to do it, which is expressed in the stark language of dispossession of the self and possession by sin: "But in fact it is no longer I that do it, but sin that dwells within me" (Rom. 7:17). The point of this stark thesis of the inevitability of sin is that every attempt at self-liberation must necessarily fail and involve us deeper in despair. It is the very character of sin that it takes over the law of action and becomes a perverted principle of action, described in the rhetorical figure of a fictional person. There is therefore a deeper layer than the actual sinful acts. That is possession by the power of sin, which disrupts and replaces the order of knowing, willing, and doing. The flesh and the spirit are mutually exclusive orientations of human life. "Flesh" does not denote the bodily instincts and the desires of the flesh but the very principle of self-existence by which humans cut themselves off from God as the source of life. "To set the mind on the flesh is death, but to set the mind on the Spirit is life and peace" (Rom. 8:7).

If liberation is to occur, it can only come from outside ourselves. And it is this liberation from without that is the cause for Paul's emphatic thanksgiving to "God through Christ, our Lord" (Rom. 7:25). But how does this liberation occur? Paul's answer points to baptism, which he interprets as dying a real death. All who have been baptized have been baptized into Christ's death (Rom. 6:3) and have been buried, "so that, just as Christ was raised by the glory of the Father, so we too might walk in newness of life" (Rom. 6:4). Baptism means that the flesh dies, and so the wages of sin is paid, and new life, grounded in Christ's resurrection, can begin. What then is the form of the new life? It is the total reorientation of life by the Spirit. "If the Spirit of him who raised Jesus from the dead dwells in you, he who raised Christ from the dead will give life to your mortal bodies also through his Spirit that dwells in you" (Rom. 8:11). This reorientation is God's work alone, which we apprehend in faith, and it offers the freedom that was lost by bondage to sin as the slaveholder.

## Making Sense of Non-Sense: The Doctrinal Debates over Sin

With these elements of the Pauline understanding of sin and its re-actualization of the narrative of the Fall, we have the main components that have decisively influenced the doctrinal debates of sin, and particularly the development of the doctrine of original sin. The challenge for doctrinal formulation consists in the fact that, on the one hand, sin must remain a contingent fact (and therefore inexplicable, nonsense), but on the other hand, it must nevertheless be comprehensible, somehow it must make sense. It is, as Karl Barth has famously said, an "impossible possibility."[8] The influence of Augustine on the understanding of sin cannot be overestimated. All following debates can be seen as a series of footnotes on Augustine's understanding of sin and grace.[9] Over against the Manicheans, and so over against his own earlier beliefs, the early Augustine emphasized, after his conversion first to Neoplatonism and then to Christianity, that sin has its origin in the free will turning away from God (*De libero arbitrio* 2.53) and that its ontological status is that of a privation of good. Already before the controversy with Pelagius, he argued (in *Ad Simplicianum*) that all humans find themselves from the beginning in a connection of sin and guilt from which they can be liberated only by God's grace. When he was later confronted in Rome with the teachings of the British monk Pelagius, who maintained that humans have free will and therefore can turn away from sinning by a radical ascetic reorientation of life, Augustine taught that the freedom not to sin is lost in the Fall since all have sinned in Adam (and not because of Adam, Rom. 5:12), and this *peccatum originale* is transmitted through sexual intercourse (*De peccatorum meritis* 1.10). Vocation, the beginning, the perseverance, and the perfection of faith are exclusively the work of divine grace and thereby effectively replace the activity of the free will (*De gratia Christi et de peccato originali*; *De nuptiis et concupiscentia*). Augustine's key concepts of the psychopathology of sin, *amor sui* (self-love), *superbia* (pride as self-elevation to the status of God), and *concupiscentia* (the desire to possess in order to compensate for the lack of being finite), have remained standard elements of the understanding of sin in the Western church. Augustine's understanding of original sin emphasizes our connectedness with one another as fallen creatures, the inability to liberate ourselves from the past, and the fact that our desires need a radical reorientation that we cannot effect by ourselves so we are radically dependent on God's grace. At least part of the conflict with Pelagius is due to Augustine's and Pelagius's different views of the soul. Whereas Pelagius was a creationist, maintaining that each soul is created afresh with the beginning of a new life and starts life unencumbered by the sins of past generations, Augustine seems to have embraced a traducianist view of the soul, according to which each soul is formed in the union of the parents and so participates in the common history of humankind as it is handed on from generation to generation. One must protect Augustine from a biologistic interpretation of his views since he does not separate nature and nurture but sees them both as interacting. If sin is to be overcome, this can be God's work alone through Christ, which is communicated to us in the objectivity of the sacraments of baptism and the Eucharist, which set us on the way to our eschatological perfection. In this life, however, as it is characterized by the struggle between the *civitas terrena* and *civitas dei*, we cannot but be involved in the *massa peccati*, as Augustine refers to sinful humanity in a curiously impersonal expression, and we can only hope that we belong to the elect, which God has chosen for eternal life.

The medieval debate is very well characterized by Thomas Aquinas's understanding of sin,[10] which in many ways developed in critical debate with Ibn Rushd's understanding of the human condition and human freedom.[11] Thomas Aquinas treats sin in the *Summa theologiae* (I-II, q. 71–89),[12] prefacing this discussion with a discussion of vices (I-II, q. 71). The systematic place of sin is not the doctrine of creation (discussed in connection with the doctrine of God in pars I) but the actualization of the human destiny (*beatitudo*). Natures are constituted by their *telos*. Inasmuch as vice is against nature, it is also against the order of reason (q. 71, a. 2r.). Since vices and sins are related according to the habit–act scheme, sin as a human act is located in the realm of the will and characterized by a lack of correspondence with the rule of reason. The rule of reason refers to both human reason and the eternal law, in a sense the reason of God (q. 71, a. 6r.). Original sin is for Thomas also a sin of nature (q. 81, a. 1r.). Adam is, in Thomas's view—which here follows the view of Adam as a corporate and representative personality that can be found in the platonic traditions but probably also in the Old Testament traditions that speak of Adam as a "corporate personality"[13]—the volitional center of humanity who moves by the motion of generation all who have their origin in him (q. 81, a. 1r.): humanity is identical in its origin but plural according to its number (q. 81, a. 2r.). Original sin is a weakening of nature (*languor naturae*, q. 82, a. 1r.); materially, it is a disorder of nature (q. 82, a. 3r.). It is the loss of original justice, a defect that can be remedied through the theological virtues that surpass the natural abilities of humans (q. 62, a. 1r.). The infusion of the theological virtues in baptism is the divine aid (*adiutorium*) that directs humans anew to their supernatural goal. Concupiscence as the *fomes peccati* is an inclination of the sensual appetite for that which is against reason (III, q. 15, a. 2), a "relic" from the state of humans before the Fall.[14] By the loss of original justice, sensual appetite becomes the capacity for producing acts that contradict charity without destroying it. As venial sins, the effects of this sensual appetite can be dealt with by the system of penitence. With regard to both original sin and the continuing concupiscence, humans depend on the penitential and sacramental system of the church to lead a Christian life. Thomas remains representative not only for trying to recover the basic outlines of an Aristotelian ethics for Christian theology but also for understanding sin and grace consistently in their relationship to human freedom, which, for Thomas, is understood as being enabled by grace to cooperate with God's will and so contribute to the actualization of God's *telos* for humanity.

A far more radical understanding of sin is then introduced by Martin Luther, whose conception of sin can be understood as a restatement of the radical points of Augustine's teaching on sin. Against the background of postulating an immediate relationship of humans to God in the late medieval mystics (Meister Eckhart, Johannes Tauler) and the nominalist tendency of allowing for the possibility of an immediate relationship of God to humans in acts of grace (cf. W. Ockham, *Quodlibeta* III, q. 10), Luther introduces, beginning already in 1513, a radicalized relational understanding of sin and grace. Sin is an offense against God, a transgression of the first commandment, which can adequately be expressed only in the language of self-accusation. This alone gives all glory to God. Not confessing one's sin means denying that Christ died for us. Original sin becomes the *peccatum radicale*, the root of sin, in the sense of the structural characteristic, which is actualized in all actual sins. The nature of sin consists in not wanting God to be God: "Non potest homo naturaliter velle deum esse deum, Immo vellet se esse deum et deum non esse deum."[15] This is starkly expressed in the second article of the Augsburg Confession: "It is also taught among us that since the fall of Adam all men who are born according to the course of nature are conceived and born in sin. That is, all men are full of evil lust and inclinations from their mothers' wombs and are unable by nature to have true faith in God. Moreover, this inborn sickness and hereditary sin is truly sin and condemns to the eternal wrath of God all those who are not born again through Baptism and the Holy Spirit."[16]

Consequently, sin can be conquered only by God's threefold divine self-giving, by means of which God's self-presentation becomes our power and aid in faith: "For by this knowledge we obtain love and delight in all the commandments of God, because here we see that God gives Himself entire to us, with all that He has and is able to do, to aid and direct us in keeping the Ten Commandments—the Father, all creatures; the Son, His entire work; and the Holy Ghost, all His gifts."[17] The consequences of this view are particularly radical with regard to the understanding of human freedom. Luther understands the freedom of the first humans before the Fall already as a bound freedom, a finite form of freedom that is dependent on God's word for its orientation. After the Fall, it has lost all capacities for even a limited self-orientation and requires complete reorientation through being illumined by the Holy Spirit to recognize the truth of the Gospel of Christ as the will of God the Creator. However, once we are relocated in relationship to God by Christ's changing places with us, we are enabled to cooperate with the will of God. There is no cooperation with God's grace for our justification, but once we are justified, we are liberated for cooperation with God. However, even then we remain bound to sin since we are justified sinners, and therefore, we have to return again and again to God's grace in the proclamation of the word and the celebration of the sacraments. Although God's justifying grace is eschatologically ultimate, and although being encumbered in sinful relationships no longer condemns us, we remain in constant battle with the flesh until we die. The process of Christian formation, the process of sanctification, therefore, is a lifelong engagement with sin and its consequences that must return at each stage to its beginning, the gift of God's grace in baptism, and remains permanently dependent on the guidance of God's Word and God's Spirit.[18]

## Changing Places: Dislocated by Sin—Relocated in Faith. A Theological Proposal

As a summary of these brief observations on the biblical discourse of sin and the brief reminders of the complex history of doctrinal debates in Western theology on the character of sin, I would like to make three suggestions for the discussion of the problems of sin.

1. The character of sin should be understood as *dislocation* of human creatures in their relationship to God the Creator. The possibility of sin is rooted in their being as images of God: humans are destined for creaturely self-determination. However, since their created will is incapable of self-orientation, humans contradict God. Original sin is an expression of the soteriological incapacity of fallen creatures. If fallen creatures could restore themselves to their original place in the relationship to God, they themselves would be godlike. The actuality of the contradiction against the Creator shapes all relationships in which humans exist and comes to expression as self-contradiction in the relationships of humans to themselves, to other people, and to the created world. If we conceive of creation as a Triune act in which the Father is the original cause, the Son the creative cause, and the Spirit the perfecting cause (cf. Basil, *De Spir.* 16.38), sin consists in claiming to be self-existent, self-creating, and self-perfecting. Claiming to be self-existent need not have the character of an explicit ontological claim; rather, it appears as the implicit ontological presupposition of claims to radical autonomy, denying the createdness of human beings, which implies both the absolute dependence on God the Creator and the co-createdness with the rest

of creation. Sin's true character is idolatry, which is as much evident in individual forms of shaping one's life as in the forms of communal living. The contradiction against God becomes apparent both as self-contradiction and as the distortion of our social relationships. Claiming to be self-creative is intrinsically bound up with the claim to be self-existent. It consists in the free self-determination of ourselves—I will be whatever I chose to be—and so denies the relative and dependent self-determination of a finite creature, entrusted with created, finite freedom. The desire to be self-perfecting can be traced throughout the course of human history and has become a dominant ideology in late modernity, whether it finds expression in the individual striving for perfection, underlying such trivial phenomena as the religious attitude with which physical or spiritual perfection is aspired to and pursued, and such disturbing phenomena as the creation of a humanity free of genetic defects, which fuels the dreams connected with genetic enhancement. However, it is important to note that sin is not only an expression of the arrogance of the dislocated creature, dreaming to be godlike, but also the denial of the full creaturely potential with which we have been endowed, the rebellion against the full actualization of all human potentialities in communion with God. The Augustinian psychopathology of sin (*superbia*, *amor sui*, *concupiscentia*) should not be restricted to phenomena of sinful self-elevation but should be extended, as Karl Barth has suggested,[19] to comprise sloth as the unwillingness of humans to strive for actualizing the full potential of becoming human, the denial of the "freedom of glory of the children of God" (Rom. 8:21). The "relational" understanding of sin is compatible with a "topical" account of sin, inspired by Michel Foucault's reflection on utopian and heterotopian spaces.[20] Foucault contrasts *utopian* places as "sites which have no real place" and stand in an "inverted relation" to the real spaces of society with heterotopias, places in various ways defined by their "otherness." One could say that in the story of the Fall, the promise of the serpent, "you will be like God," points to such a "utopian place" that has no real location in the order of creation. Humans follow this promise, take the *utopia* for real, and thus are displaced in the order of creation. The garden is no longer home for them, and they must establish their life "east of Eden" under difficult circumstances. Following the utopian promise, they find themselves in a *heterotopia*. This seems to be characteristic for sin in general in striving for the utopian places; the real world becomes difficult and hostile because the effects of sin turn it in relation to the original place of human creatures into a *heterotopos*.

2. The liberation from sin and the forgiveness of the sinner consists in the separation of sinners from their sins through God's judgment. Sinners are relocated in their relationship to God by God taking their place of dislocation in Christ and so effecting what Luther called the "joyous exchange" by offering

sinful humans as God's daughters and sons Christ's place in a filial relationship to God through the Spirit. Christ's obedient acceptance of the place of sinful humanity is expressed by Luther in the most drastic ways. Following the logic of 2 Corinthians 5:21—"For our sake he [God] made him [Christ] to be sin who knew of no sin"—he portrays God as declaring to Christ: "You shall be Peter the denier, Paul, the persecutor, the blasphemer and violent character, David, the adulterer and that sinner who took the apple in paradise, the robber on the cross, you shall be the person of all humans who has committed all their sins."[21] As Christ bears the sins of all humanity in his death on the cross, liberation from all sins is achieved: "After that was done [Jesus's death] the whole world is liberated from sins and death by this one man."[22] Christians are called on to celebrate the absolution of all sins, which are no longer in the world since Christ has taken them on himself, offering his place in the relationship to God the Father to all sinners who have been liberated from their sins. This relocation in the relationship to God extends to all relationships in which humans exist. The sinner becomes a justified sinner, for whom God's forgiveness becomes self-acceptance and for whom the world is not "vanity fair" but the *theatrum gloriae Dei*, the "theater of God's glory." In "topical" form, Christ identifies in the Incarnation and especially in his death on the cross with the *heterotopos*—the place of displacement, the place of death—as the divine critique of the human "utopian" projection, and so makes this *heterotopos* the *theotopos*, the place where God wants to be known. In every communion service the consequences of this joyous exchange are reenacted, reenacted by Christ himself, offering sinners a place in communion with God; it is a taking leave of "utopian" dreams and being led in an exodus from the *heterotopos* of life in estrangement from God into life in the communion of God and God's reconciled creation. In a communion service, believers are liberated from the *heterochrony* of a life, dominated by the past through the effects of sin. In the promise of forgiveness, their lives are synchronized with the *theochrony* that shapes the story of the world from creation to the eschatological fulfillment.

3. Following this proposal, the question of the knowledge of sin should therefore be answered in the following way: All humans have an indistinct vague awareness of sin (*notitia peccati*). Being confronted with the will of God (law), they can have knowledge of sin (*cognitio peccati*), including their own incapacity to liberate themselves from bondage to sin. By being addressed through the Gospel of Christ, sinful humans can acknowledge sin as their own sin (*recognitio peccati*).[23] This has its place in the first-person language of the confession of sin, the only adequate form of discourse about sin, which is enabled by the promise of divine grace.

## Notes

1 Cf. Gerhard Schulze, *Die Sünde. Das schöne Leben und seine Feinde* (Munich: Carl Hanser, 2006); and Aviad Kleinberg, *Seven Deadly Sins: A Very Partial List* (Cambridge, MA: Harvard University Press, 2010).

2 For an extensive conversation on sin, judgment, and grace by Christian and Muslim theologians, see the chapter "Verfehlung und Barmherzigkeit; Sünde, Gericht, Gnade" by Susanne Heine, Mouhanad Khorchide, Yasar Sarikaya, and Christoph Schwöbel, in *Christen und Muslime im Gespräch. Eine Verständigung über Kernthemen der Theologie*, ed. Susanne Heine, Ömer Öszoy, Christoph Schwöbel, and Abdullah Takim (Gütersloh: Gütersloher Verlagshaus, 2014), 125–53.

3 Cf. Rolf Knierim, *Die Hauptbegriffe für Sünde im Alten Testament*, 2nd ed. (Gütersloh: Gütersloher Verlagshaus, 1967). An excellent discussion is provided in Bernd Janowski, *Ein Gott, der straft und tötet? Zwölf Fragen zum Gottesbild des Alten Testaments* (Neukirchen: Neukirchener Verlagshaus, 2013), 232–60.

4 In this account of the understanding of sin in the writings of the New Testament, I have learned most from the excellent survey in Michael Wolter, "Die Rede von der Sünde im Neuen Testament," in *Sünde*, ed. Wilfried Härle and Reiner Preul, Marburger Jahrbuch Theologie XX (Leipzig: Evangelische Verlagsanstalt, 2008), 15–44.

5 It is mentioned for the first time in the story of Cain. When Cain gets angry because God had regard for Abel's offering but not for his own offering, the story tells us, God questions and warns Cain: "Why are you angry, and why has your countenance fallen? If you do well, will you not be accepted? And if you do not well, sin is lurking at the door; its desire is for you, but you must master it" (Gen. 4:6–7). It is significant that the first terminological mention of sin does not refer to an act, a habit, or a disposition but rather depicts sin as a quasi-personal power at work in the affective life of Cain.

6 Cf. Christoph Schwöbel, "Imago Libertatis: Human and Divine Freedom," in *God and Freedom*, ed. Colin E. Gunton (Edinburgh: T&T Clark, 1995), 57–81.

7 Cf. Christoph Schwöbel, "Human Being as Relational Being: Twelve Theses for a Christian Anthropology," in *Persons, Divine and Human*, ed. Christoph Schwöbel and Colin Gunton (Edinburgh: T&T Clark, 1991), 141–79.

8 Cf., for a careful exposition of this phrase, Nicholas Wolterstorff, "Barth on Evil," *Faith and Philosophy* 13 (1996): 584–608.

9 For an informative discussion covering most of the extensive literature, cf. Jesse Couenhoven, "St. Augustine's Doctrine of Original Sin," *Augustinian Studies* 36, no. 2 (2005): 359–96. On the philosophical problem, see the illuminating account of Robert Merrihew Adams, "Original Sin: A Study in the Interaction of Philosophy and Theology," in *The Question of Christian Philosophy Today*, ed. Francis J. Ambrosio (New York: Fordham University Press, 1998), 80–110.

10 On the medieval debates, cf. the instructive study by Volker Leppin, "Aristotelisierung, Immediatisierung und Radikalisierung. Transformationen der Sündenlehre von Thomas von Aquin bis Martin Luther," in Härle and Preul, *Sünde*, 45–73. Leppin points

to the continuities between the medieval mystical and nominalist theologies and Luther's theology. While in Thomas Aquinas the relationship between God and humanity appears mediated through the Aristotelian categories, focusing on the questions how humans can achieve their divinely posited *telos* so that sin is discussed in an anthropological context, the late medieval mystics and important nominalist theologians assumed a direct mystical encounter with God in grace that could lead also to a more theological understanding of sin. This view is radicalized by Luther in such a way that sin is the direct turning away from God and thereby rebelling against God. The effect of this turning away is pervasive and affects all dimensions of human existence. The disruption in the relationship between God and sinful humanity is so severe that humans who are condemned to death can be saved only by the exclusive divine act of grace in Christ, who takes the place of sinful humanity in order to share his place in relationship to God the Father with the believers who have been justified by God's grace alone.

11 For an illuminating discussion on the "triangle" of Ibn Rushd, Maimonides, and Thomas Aquinas, see David B. Burrell, *Freedom and Creation in Three Traditions* (Notre Dame, IN: University of Notre Dame Press, 1994); and David B. Burrell, *Faith and Freedom: An Interfaith Perspective* (Oxford: Wiley-Blackwell, 2004).

12 *St. Thomas Aquinas Summa Theologica*, trans. Fathers of the English Dominican Province (Westminster, MD: Christian Classics, 1981), vol. 2 (I-II, q. 1–114), 895–990.

13 Cf. H. Wheeler Robinson, *Corporate Personality in Ancient Israel*, rev. ed. (Edinburgh: T. & T. Clark, 1981). While this concept has been contended, the elements that it comprises remained influential throughout the history of Jewish and Christian thought: the identification of an individual with a group and of a group with an individual; the extension of the individual to comprehend those who are related to that individual; the fact that these relations are regarded as real; and the possibility of going back and forth between individual and social characteristics. Much of that could be rephrased by talking of the representative relationality of people.

14 *St. Thomas Aquinas Summa Theologica*, vol. 4, 2100. This definition of concupiscence as *fomes peccati* as the trigger of sin, the selfish human desire for an object, person, or experience that can be actualized in sin but, according to Catholic teaching, is not to be equated with sin, is placed in the discussion of the Incarnation and the "sinlessness" of Christ. According to Catholic teaching, human nature has not been completely corrupted by the Fall but has been wounded and weakened. Apart from ignorance and the domination by death, there is also an inclination toward evil and sin (see *The Catechism of the Catholic Church* 405, 418). According to the Reformers, concupiscence as the summary name for the desires leading to sin must itself be regarded as sinful. The Reformers also maintain that human nature may not be called substantially evil because it is created by God, but it is as a whole perverted by sin. For the Reformers, sin cannot be adequately described in terms of a privation, a deficiency that is the result of the Fall, but must be seen as a perversion, resulting from being wholly in the wrong in relation to God. This finds its expression in their view of sinners being curved on themselves (*incurvatus in se ipsum*), not open to the address of God.

15 Martin Luther, *Disputatio contra scholasticam theologiam* 1517, WA 1, 225,1.

16 The Augsburg Confession, art. 2, in *The Book of Concord*, trans. and ed. Theodore G. Tappert (Philadelphia: Fortress Press, 1959), 29.

17 Martin Luther, *Large Catechism*, The Creed 3. art. 69, in *The Book of Concord*, 420.

18 The statement that justified sinners are *simul iustus, simul peccator*, at the same time justified and sinners, is one of the points where the teaching of the Reformers is puzzling to Catholics and Orthodox Christians alike. Its main intention is to secure that those who are justified are indeed the sinners. The new humanity is the old humanity, as it is restored and re-created by God's grace. Only after our death will we, according to the Reformers, be wholly transformed by the grace of God. There is, from my perspective, a striking similarity to this contentious point in Reformation theology in Catholic and Orthodox spirituality: the saints, although they are seen as illuminating examples of the transforming power of God's grace, regard themselves as sinners, as unworthy of God's favor, let alone the veneration of humans.

19 Cf. Karl Barth, *Church Dogmatics IV/2: The Doctrine of Reconciliation* (London: T&T Clark International, 2004), 403–83.

20 Michel Foucault, "Of Other Spaces," trans. Jay Miskowiec, in *Diacritics* 16, no. 1 (1986): 22–27.

21 WA 40/1, 437, 23–26.

22 WA 40/1, 438, 1–2.

23 For a more extensive argument for this view, cf. Christoph Schwöbel, "Sünde—Selbstwiderspruch im Widerspruch gegen Gott. Annäherungen an das Verständnis eines christlichen Zentralbegriffs," in *Gott im Gespräch. Theologische Studien zur Gegenwartsdeutung* (Tübingen: Mohr Siebeck, 2011), 291–320.

# The Concept of Sin in the Qur'ān in Light of the Story of Adam

AYMAN SHABANA

**SIN IS** a loaded and multivalent term. It is hard to translate and even harder to discuss in an interfaith context because of its different semantic and theological connotations in different religious traditions. Nonetheless, given its centrality in both the Qur'ān and the Bible, it offers an opportunity for thoughtful reflection on how Muslims and Christians perceive this concept in light of their scripture. In this essay I examine the Qur'ānic concept of sin in light of the story of Adam as an illustrative example of how sin has been conceptualized in the Islamic exegetical and theological traditions. Given the selected passages in this seminar, I will focus on three main points: sin in the Qur'ānic story of Adam, particularly in Sūrat al-Aʿrāf (7):10–27; the conceptualization of sin in the Islamic exegetical and theological traditions; and the relationship between sin and the (lower) self (*nafs*), particularly in light of al-Aʿrāf (7):177–79 and Yūsuf (12):18 and 53.

## Disambiguation of Sin

In Arabic several terms are associated with the concept of sin, and each of them refers to one of its possible meanings. At least three main senses can be distinguished in the Islamic normative tradition. The first is sin as disobedience in the broadest sense, which is associated with Arabic terms such as *maʿṣiya* and *ʿiṣyān* and their various derivatives.[1] The second is sin as an ethico-moral wrong and can be translated as *khaṭīʾa*, *ithm*, *dhanb*, or *sayyiʾa*.[2] This sense covers the notion of a bad or evil deed. Sometimes the word for evil (*sharr*) is also used in this sense. One useful way to trace these different terms in the Qur'ān is to examine them in combination with their antonyms. For example, the opposite of *maʿṣiya* is *ṭāʿa*, which itself occurs only three times in the Qur'ān (al-Nisāʾ [4]:81; al-Nūr

[24]:53; Muḥammad [47]:21), although several other verbal derivatives are used repeatedly.[3] The word *sayyi'a* (pl. *sayyi'āt*) is often contrasted with its antonym *ḥasana* (pl. *ḥasanāt*).[4] Similarly, the word *sharr* (evil) is contrasted with its antonym *khayr*, as in al-Zalzala (99):7–8. Occasionally, some of these terms are combined, as is the case in al-Nisā' (4):112, where the terms *khaṭī'a* and *ithm* are combined, but more often they are contrasted with their opposites. The term *sayyi'a* is particularly important because it denotes moral wrong, which both causes misfortune and incurs punishment. The third sense is associated with ethico-legal infractions, or *ḥudūd*, which stand for crimes with stipulated punishments, such as adultery and murder. Terms such as *fāḥisha* and *faḥshā'* are used for this type of sin, as is the case in al-Isrā' (17):32, where the former is used to refer to adultery.

These three senses are not mutually exclusive; they tend to overlap at least at certain levels. For example, a *ḥadd* is an infraction in the Islamic legal sense because it has a stipulated punishment in this world according to Sharī'a, but the word also signifies the act of disobeying God's command, which is a religious sin. This overlap is the reason *ḥudūd* are categorized as belonging to the domain of either God's rights or the mixed rights of God and man. They involve God's rights as far as violation of the divine command is concerned. Similarly, they involve man's rights as far as encroachment on other people's rights is concerned. On the other hand, a *ma'ṣiya* or *dhanb* involves disobedience but might not have a worldly punishment. Punishment for sin in this sense is relegated to God in the hereafter.

One of the most famous classifications of sin in the Islamic normative tradition is the division into major (*kabīra*, pl. *kabā'ir*) and minor (*ṣaghīra*, pl. *ṣaghā'ir*) sins. The term *kabā'ir* is mentioned in the Qur'ān in Sūrat al-Nisā' (4):31, where it is indicated that avoidance of major sins could provide grounds for the forgiveness of other (minor) sins. In his commentary Muḥammad b. Jarīr al-Ṭabarī discusses the different interpretations of the term *kabā'ir*, some of which specify a certain number of major sins while others allow for more open-ended definitions. For example, according to one view, which is authenticated by several successors to the Companion 'Abd Allāh ibn Mas'ūd, *kabā'ir* include all the condemned practices mentioned in the thirty verses of al-Nisā' preceding the verse in which the term is mentioned.[5] Another definition, also attributed to Ibn Mas'ūd, specifies four major sins: associating partners with God, despairing God's forgiveness (*al-qunūṭ min raḥmat Allāh*), losing hope in God's mercy (*al-ya's min rawḥ Allāh*), and feeling security from God's plotting (*al-amn min makr Allāh*).[6] According to another view, attributed to 'Alī ibn Abī Ṭālib, the major sins are seven in number: associating partners with God, committing murder, committing slander, usurping an orphan's property, consuming usury, fleeing from the battlefield, and leading a

Bedouin lifestyle after Hijra (immigration to Medina). All these sins are also mentioned separately in the Qur'ān.[7] According to a variant definition, attributed to Ibn ʿUmar, the major sins are nine: associating partners with God, committing murder, fleeing from the battlefield, committing slander, consuming usury, usurping an orphan's property, causing mischief in the holy mosque, performing black magic, and feeling ingratitude for one's parents.[8] In addition, Ibn ʿAbbās reportedly asserted that all the deeds that God warned against constitute major sins, especially those against which the punishment of Fire is stipulated. Ibn ʿAbbās is also reported to have said, "No major sins with repentance, and no minor sins with insistence" (*lā kabīrah maʿa istighfār, wa-lā ṣaghīrah maʿa iṣrār*).[9] Al-Ṭabarī also points out several prophetic reports that refer to major sins and that tend to reiterate most of the sins previously mentioned: associating partners with God, feeling ingratitude for one's parents, committing murder, making false statements (testimony), committing slander, taking false oaths, practicing magic, fleeing from the battlefield, and committing adultery.[10]

## Master Narrative on Sin in the Qur'ān

One of the main stories explaining the concept of sin in the Qur'ān is that of Adam. This story is filled with religious and spiritual meaning on a wide range of issues, such as human creation, the God–man relationship, and the human condition as well as human destiny. Several passages in different chapters refer to particular aspects of the story, sometimes reinforcing certain points or highlighting new dimensions. The story concentrates on man's capacity to rise to virtue, characterized here as obedience to God's command, or fall into sin, characterized as disobedience.

The passage in al-Aʿrāf (7):11–27 concentrates on the encounter between Iblīs and both Adam and his wife. Like the passage in al-Baqara (2):30–39, it also alludes to the divine honor bestowed upon Adam and his progeny by the instruction given to the angels to prostrate themselves before him. Each of these passages has its own specific features, details, and points of emphasis. The Qur'ānic narrative of Adam in these two passages, and others throughout the Qur'ān, involves some important themes, such as the creation of man by God's hands (Ṣād [38]:75); the breathing of His spirit into him (Ṣād [38]:72); the rationale for God's creative acts; the infiniteness of God's knowledge and wisdom; human dignity, which stems from the divine honor bestowed on Adam and through him on humanity; damnation of Iblīs and eternal enmity with man; possibility of renewal through repentance; and finally the paradox and mystery of human nature.[11] All these themes have been the subject of endless debate among the different theological schools.

School boundaries have in fact been constructed on the basis of views on issues such as divine anthropomorphism, human freedom and ability to act independently, predestination, and, most important for the present context, the status of a sinner and the impact of sin on one's standing as a believer.

In al-Aʿrāf (7):11–27, the main focus is on Iblīs's disobedience of the divine command and his temptation of both Adam and his wife. The Qurʾān uses two terms to refer to the devil: *iblīs* and *shayṭān*. The first denotes desperateness and revolt, and the second denotes active wrongdoing, perversity, and incitement. The context makes the distinction clear: the first term is used to refer to the refusal to obey the divine command to bow before Adam, and the second is used in reference to Iblīs's attempt to seduce Adam and his wife.[12] The passage begins with the divine act of human creation and shaping; the angels are ordered to bow before the human creature by virtue of his being the recipient of divine attention and consideration. Iblīs, however, disregards this point and concentrates rather on the human creature's substance in comparison to his own allegedly higher nature. Iblīs refuses to obey the order and justifies his attitude by pointing out his superiority over Adam, which lies in the difference between clay and fire. Iblīs is rebuked and banished because of his insolence, pride, and arrogance. Because he fails to comply with the divine command, Iblīs is denounced and damned. He is driven out of paradise and commanded to descend from this place that is reserved for only the faithful ones. Iblīs asks for a respite until the day of resurrection, which is granted not to fix his mistake but to mislead and misguide others away from the straight path and divine guidance. The commentators note that Iblīs's efforts at seduction are meant to test people's commitment to the divine command and verify their ability to resist and withstand temptation. People are similarly tested by all types of worldly pleasures and attractions as well as different desires ingrained in their nature and lower selves.

The passage then turns to focus on Adam, who was instructed, together with his wife, to dwell in the Garden, where they can enjoy all the available bounties with the exception of the fruit from one tree. Iblīs, however, tells Adam and his wife that the forbidden tree is the tree of angelhood and eternity. Upon eating from the forbidden tree, the two realize their mistake; they become aware of their nakedness and feel a great sense of shame. They acknowledge their wrongdoing and call on God to forgive them. They are commanded to descend from the Garden and told that for a certain term their abode will be on Earth, where they will be in a state of enmity with Iblīs. The passage then addresses the children of Adam by pointing out ways of covering nakedness but further explains that God-consciousness is the best guard against sin, which was the root cause of the first couple's sense of shame. The passage concludes with an admonition addressed to the children of Adam to beware of Iblīs and to guard against repeating the mistake of their (first) parents.

## The Story of Adam in the *Tafsīr* Literature

Perhaps the most important feature in the Qur'ānic story of Adam, and indeed Qur'ānic narratives in general, is its brevity and conciseness. A cursory comparison of the Qur'ānic narrative and the biblical one will immediately reveal the difference in the level of detail in each of them. For example, as far as the story of Adam is concerned, the Qur'ān does not specify the location of the Garden, the type of the tree from which the couple was forbidden to eat, the exact way Iblīs seduced them, and the exact place to which they descended from the Garden.[13] The Qur'ān's focus on the main lines of the narrative rather than the minute details has prompted commentators to pursue these details since the early works of Qur'ānic exegesis.

The most important sources that the early generations of commentators relied on in answering open questions about the Qur'ānic narratives were the People of the Book, and this reliance on outside sources marked the beginning of a debate on the role, significance, and, most important, the authority of biblical narratives. The term used for such (primarily Jewish) literature is *isrā'īliyyāt*. Although several well-regarded ḥadīths make up commentaries on passages in the Qur'ān, most of the reports in this genre are believed to be unreliable to the extent that Aḥmad ibn Ḥanbal is reported to have said that three genres are of questionable foundations (*laysa lahā aṣl*): the exegetical narratives (*tafsīr*), legendary poetry (*malāḥim*), and narratives concerning battles (*maghāzī*).[14]

Exploring the expansive *tafsīr* literature throughout the Islamic tradition falls beyond the scope of the present essay.[15] I will, however, refer briefly to the two main approaches often used in surveying this extended tradition: historical and typological. The historical approach examines the exegetical tradition along its main stages of historical development (e.g., formative, classical, mature, and contemporary).[16] The typological approach concentrates instead on the main classifications of *tafsīr* works regardless of the historical context within which these works were developed. The most important example is the binary classification of report-based exegesis (*riwāyah/ma'thūr*) and opinion-based exegesis (*ra'y/dirāyah*).[17] For report-based *tafsīr*, I will concentrate on the famous work by Ibn Jarīr al-Ṭabarī (d. 310/923).[18] For the opinion-based *tafsīr*, I will concentrate on the famous work by Fakhr al-Dīn al-Rāzī (d. 606/1209). For an example of an exegetical work in the modern period, I will concentrate on *Tafsīr al-Manār* of Muḥammad 'Abduh (d. 1905) and Muḥammad Rashīd Riḍā (d. 1935).[19]

Al-Ṭabarī's commentary is considered one of the main early works of *tafsīr* that are based on the extant reports in his time. Scholars, however, recognize that it is not merely a compilation of related exegetical reports; it is as well "a carefully structured work which evinces considerable insight and judgment."[20] Its importance and significance can be traced in all the subsequent works of *tafsīr* from the time of its composition to the present day. Similarly, the *tafsīr* of al-Rāzī is considered one of the most important works of *tafsīr* by opinion. It draws on the full spectrum of the Islamic intellectual tradition, particularly theology and philosophy. Although al-Rāzī is one of the prominent followers of the Ashʿarī school of theology, he also often relates the opinions of other schools, mainly Muʿtazilī, in his vindication of the opinion of his school. Al-Rāzī's work, like al-Ṭabarī's, has also been one of the main resources that subsequent works of *tafsīr* drew on. *Tafsīr al-Manār* offers a good example of a work that seeks to interpret the Qurʾān in the spirit of the modern period and that also seeks to maintain its currency and appeal to reason and rationality. This commentary was delivered by the famous Egyptian reformer Muḥammad ʿAbduh in the form of lectures at al-Azhar Mosque in Cairo. It was initially published by his disciple Rashīd Riḍā in *Majallat al-Manār* and was later collected and published separately, containing ʿAbduh's lectures as captured by Riḍā as well as the latter's own comments on those lectures. Although this commentary does not cover the entire Qurʾān (it extends only until Yūsuf [12]:52), it has become one of the most important commentaries on the Qurʾān in the modern period.

This sample is selective and in many ways arbitrary. However, it still allows us to explore the various methods used by the authors of *tafsīr* works in their commentary on the meaning and significance of the story of Adam, especially as far as the notion of sin is concerned. All these works belong to mainstream Sunnism as it developed historically. Many other types of *tafsīr* works could have been included in both the premodern and modern periods either on the basis of typology, such as works with emphasis on Sufism, philosophy, or jurisprudence, or on the basis of religious or theological orientation, such as works by Shīʿis or other sects falling beyond mainstream Sunnism.[21] In the following I highlight some points and themes that reflect the perspective of each of these works.

## Al-Ṭabarī and Report-Based Exegesis

One of the main questions that occupied the Qurʾān commentators from the early period was about the nature of Iblīs and whether he belonged to the angels. In one verse (al-Kahf [18]:50) the Qurʾān indicates that Iblīs belonged to the jinn, which raises a question about the relationship between the angels and the jinn. If the angels and the jinn are two different species, how was it that Iblīs was allowed among the angels when the command was given to prostrate before Adam? Al-Ṭabarī references a report attributed to Ibn ʿAbbās that seeks to answer these questions. According to this report, Iblīs belonged to a group of angels called jinn, who were created out of fire.[22] His name was al-Ḥārith, and he was one of the guards of paradise. The other angels were created out of light. The other jinn mentioned in the Qur'ān were created out of smokeless fire, and Adam was created out of clay. The jinn were the first to inhabit the Earth, but they caused mischief and bloodshed. God sent Iblīs along with an army of the angels to which he belonged, and they defeated the jinn and drove them to the islands of the sea and the outer rims of the mountains. Iblīs was proud of his achievement and thought no one else could have driven the jinn away. When God learned how Iblīs felt, He decided to test him by creating Adam and commanding Iblīs and his kind to prostrate before Adam.[23] According to this report, God's discourse on the creation of a viceroy on Earth in al-Baqara (2):30 is addressed to the specific group of angels to which Iblīs belonged, not to all the angels. Iblīs and the others questioned the wisdom of creating a viceroy who could cause corruption and bloodshed like the earlier jinn whom they had defeated.[24]

Al-Ṭabarī also references another report, attributed to Ibn ʿAbbās, Ibn Masʿūd, and a number of other Companions, according to which Iblīs was one of the guards of paradise who was given the dominion of the heaven of this world. When arrogance entered Iblīs's heart, God decided to test him by the creation of Adam.[25] According to this report, God told the angels (all the angels, not only the group to which Iblīs belonged) that this being could have progeny who would cause corruption and bloodshed. The angels questioned why God would create such a being when he had the angels to glorify and worship Him.[26] The response from God emphasizes His all-embracing knowledge: He knows what the angels do not know.[27] God knew about Iblīs and his arrogance, and He knew that not all the progeny of Adam would be prone to corruption and bloodshed.[28] Other reports that al-Ṭabarī records indicate that the creation of Adam was meant to be a test for the angels, who thought that they were the best creatures and that God would not favor anyone over them.[29]

Turning to Adam and his wife, al-Ṭabarī records a report, attributed to Ibn ʿAbbās, Ibn Masʿūd, and other Companions, that indicates Adam's admission into the Garden after Iblīs had been expelled from it but before he was sent down to Earth because of his arrogance and insolence.[30] The Qur'ān does not mention how Adam's wife was created, but al-Ṭabarī, relying on reports by Ibn ʿAbbās, Ibn Masʿūd, and other Companions, describes how Eve was created from Adam's rib.[31] Similarly, he records several opinions on the type of tree from which the couple was forbidden to eat, including grain, olive, wheat, grape, and fig. He does not, however, support any of these opinions and concludes that if there were a reason to specify this type of information, God would have provided it.[32]

The Qur'ān says that Iblīs seduced Adam and his wife by whispering (al-Aʿrāf [7]:20) and by coaxing them to commit the sin of disobedience that caused their expulsion from the Garden (al-Baqara [2]:36). The Qur'ān, however, does not specify how this seduction took place. Al-Ṭabarī records reports, attributed to Wahb ibn Munabbih, Ibn ʿAbbās, and others, indicating that Iblīs was able to enter the Garden through the mouth of the serpent. He first approached Eve and incited her to eat from the forbidden tree, and later she approached Adam and incited him to do the same.[33] Al-Ṭabarī mentions that Ibn Isḥāq opined that the encounter between Adam and Iblīs could have been similar to the encounter between Iblīs and all the children of Adam—namely, it could have been indirect—but al-Ṭabarī supports the report of Wahb ibn Munabbih and Ibn ʿAbbās on several grounds. First, the absence of verified counterreports supports the plausibility of the reports of the people of knowledge (*ahl al-ʿilm*). Second, nothing in these reports can be seen as rationally impossible (*lā yadfaʿuhu ʿaql*). Third, the Qur'ān refers to a direct encounter between Iblīs on the one hand and Adam and his wife on the other, which is understood from the term *wa-qāsamahumā* (and he swore to them). In other words, a term indicating swearing would not be appropriate to describe the regular indirect encounter between Iblīs and the children of Adam.[34]

Adam and Eve immediately became aware of the consequences of their disobedience when they realized their nakedness (al-Aʿrāf [7]:22). As for the cover they had before their disobedience, several opinions are given, which include nails, light, and God-consciousness.[35] They now tried to cover themselves with the tree leaves from the Garden. Al-Ṭabarī records reports by Ibn ʿAbbās, Ubayy ibn Kaʿb, Wahb ibn Munabbih, and others that describe how Adam and Eve tried to hide and how God rebuked them for eating from the forbidden tree. Adam and Eve admitted their mistake and asked for forgiveness (al-Aʿrāf [7]:23), which is also described in al-Baqara (2):38 as a form of divine inspiration. This admission marks the main difference between the attitude of Iblīs and the attitude of Adam. Whereas the former asked for respite, the latter asked for forgiveness. The Qur'ān indicates that they each got what they asked for.[36]

The passage concludes by shifting the focus from Adam and his wife to the children of Adam and their eternal struggle with Iblīs and his followers. In al-Aʿrāf (7):26–27, the Qur'ān emphasizes God's favor on the children of Adam by granting them means to cover their bodies and to beautify themselves. According to al-Ṭabarī, the verse references the pre-Islamic Arabian habit of naked circumambulation of the shrine in Mecca.[37] Through this practice Iblīs was able to seduce the children of Adam, as he did earlier with Adam and his wife. In both cases nakedness is associated with the act of disobedience. The verses indicate that human beings need to stay on guard in their eternal battle with Iblīs.

## Al-Rāzī and Opinion-Based Exegesis

Turning to the commentary of Fakhr al-Dīn al-Rāzī, one immediately realizes the different nature of the work and the approach of its author. Al-Rāzī's commentary is well-known for its encyclopedic scope and its theological and philosophical sophistication. It clearly reflects a more developed stage in the Islamic intellectual tradition and gives expression to mature philosophical and theological arguments. The main distinction between al-Ṭabarī's commentary and al-Rāzī's is the methodological approach. Whereas the former relies mainly on traditions and reports, the latter occasionally refers to some of these traditions and reports but primarily draws on many other resources. This reliance on other resources is illustrated in al-Rāzī's commentary on the story of Adam, which is interpreted within the larger context of Islamic theological debates. As one of the main spokespersons of later Ashʿarism, al-Rāzī often vindicates the views of the Ashʿarī school against its rivals, especially the Muʿtazilites.

Al-Rāzī begins his commentary on the passage narrating the story of Adam in al-Aʿrāf (7):11–27 by examining the order of the actions mentioned at the beginning of the passage (creation, shaping, command to the angels to prostrate themselves before Adam). These actions are expressed in the plural form (*khlaqnākum thumma ṣawwarnākum*), which raises the question, is the addressee Adam or humanity? Al-Rāzī records four interpretations of this verse. The first is that Adam is the one being addressed in this context by virtue of the fact that he was the first human and is also considered the father of humanity. This is the view that al-Ṭabarī supports and that al-Rāzī describes as the commonly chosen view (*wa huwa al-mukhtār*).[38] The second is that Adam is the one who was created and his progeny were shaped in his loins before the angels were commanded to prostrate themselves before him. The third is that the command to the angels is conveyed as a report of an event that happened in the past. The order of the actions in the verse does not, however, reflect the order of their actual occurrence. The meaning would then be "We created and shaped you and recall We commanded the angels to prostrate themselves before Adam." The fourth view, which al-Rāzī supports, is that the term *creation* (*khalq*) refers to God's decree (*taqdīr*), or His foreknowledge and His will that give accurate measure for everything. Accordingly, God's creation consists of His command and will (*ḥukmuhu wa-mashīʾtuh*) to bring people into this world, and his shaping consists of documenting all things to be until the Day of Judgment in the Preserved Tablet (*al-Lawḥ al-*

*Maḥfūẓ*). Subsequent to these two actions came the creation of Adam and the command to the angels to prostrate themselves before him.[39] Elsewhere in his commentary on al-Baqara (2):34, al-Rāzī indicates, with reference also to Ṣad (38):72, that the prostration occurred before the completion of the creation of Adam. According to the latter verse, by the time Adam came into existence, the angels had already prostrated themselves before him.[40]

Al-Rāzī notes that the unanimous view among the commentators is that the prostration by the angels is not meant as worship since this would amount to disbelief, which God would not command. The commentators, however, disagreed on the exact meaning and significance of prostration. According to one view, God is the one to whom the angels prostrated, and Adam served only as a *qiblah* (prayer direction) of prostration. According to another view, prostration is meant to show respect and honor, not worship, and this is the preferred view. According to a third view, prostration signifies submission and servitude.[41]

Al-Rāzī also examines the question of whether Iblīs belonged to the angels. He explains the two main views on this issue as well as the supporting arguments for each. According to the first view, Iblīs did belong to the angels since he was among them. According to the second view, however, he did not belong to the angels owing to the many differences between the angels and the jinn. Al-Rāzī, however, does not seem to support either of these two views but concludes with a statement that indicates the feasibility of both views and relegates knowledge of the matter to God (*wa-Allāhu aʿlamu bi-ḥaqāʾiq al-umūr*). What is interesting to note here is that al-Rāzī's exposition focuses on linguistic, theological, and rational arguments. He also appeals to other verses in the Qurʾān to emphasize certain points. Although he occasionally refers to the reports that al-Ṭabarī records, these reports are not usually the main evidence that he uses to substantiate his arguments.[42]

Al-Rāzī observes that al-Aʿrāf (7):12–18 describes what seems to have been a conversation between God and Iblīs. He seeks to reconcile the view that a direct encounter with God amounts to bestowal of honor and dignity, as is the case with Moses, but this is not the case with Iblīs. He records the opinion that God did not address Iblīs directly but through angels because God did not speak directly to anyone except the prophets. According to another view, however, God may have addressed Iblīs directly, but it was in a humiliating and demeaning manner as understood from the context.[43]

Regarding whether the garden mentioned in the story is the Garden of Eden or a different one, either in heaven or on Earth, al-Rāzī records several views, including the one that al-Ṭabarī referred to, namely, that it is the Garden of Eden. Al-Rāzī notes that this is the view of the majority of our Companions (*jumhūr aṣḥābinā*) because the term used in the story (*al-janna*; see, e.g., al-Baqara [2]:35, al-A'rāf [7]:19) is the same as the one used to refer to the Garden of the Hereafter. Moreover, the term is prefaced by the definite article *al*, which denotes reference to an already known entity (*lil-'ahd*). In addition to this view, al-Rāzī mentioned three other views. According to the first one, attributed to Abū al-Qāsim al-Balkhī and Abū Muslim al-Iṣfahānī, this garden was on Earth. They interpret the word *descend* (*ihbiṭū*) to mean moving from one place to another, as it is used in al-Baqara (2):61. Several arguments are used in support of this view. First, because Adam was driven out of it, it could not be the Garden of Eden, which is meant to be an eternal abode. Also, Iblīs would not have been able to enter the Garden of Eden after he had disobeyed God. The second view is that this garden was in the seventh heaven, and since the term *descend* appears twice, in al-Baqara (2):36 and 38, the first refers to descent from the seventh heaven to the first and the second to the descent from the first to Earth. The third view is that any of these opinions could be possible because the textual references are not unequivocal. According to this view, suspension of judgment (*tawaqquf*) is the preferred attitude. Although al-Rāzī does not explicitly indicate this, it may be understood that this last view is his own.[44]

Al-Rāzī further explores the nature of the divine command to Adam to avoid eating from the forbidden tree. Was this command meant as an obligation, in which case disobedience would amount to the commission of a prohibited act; or was it optional, in which case disobedience would result in mere disapproval? Al-Rāzī notes that two views have been expressed. According to the first, the divine inhibition here was an obligation in view of the punishment that followed Adam's disobedience, that is, his expulsion from the Garden. According to the second view, the inhibition was optional; commission of the prohibited action would amount to a mere infraction (i.e., leaving a better course of action, *tark al-awlā*). Al-Rāzī supports the second view because it is more fitting for protecting the status of prophets.[45] I will come back to this point in the subsequent section on the theological implications of the story.

As for the manner in which Iblīs whispered to Adam and his wife, as mentioned in al-A'rāf 7:20, al-Rāzī does not support the report in which the serpent is mentioned, and he describes it as weak or prosaic (*rakīkah*).[46] He rather suggests that Iblīs was able to convince the couple because he tried repeatedly to do so and ultimately overwhelmed them with all types of distractions, causing them to forget the divine instruction.[47]

## *Tafsīr al-Manār* and Modern Sensibilities

The most important features of *Tafsīr al-Manār* are its concern with the relevance of the Qur'ān in the modern context and its ability to answer emerging questions. ʿAbduh's approach in this work emphasizes the Qurʾān's appeal to reason as one of the important tools for understanding both the divine written text and God's signs in the world. This approach can be explored in his remarks on the two notions of history and science. For ʿAbduh, all the past incidents mentioned in the Qurʾān are meant to emphasize moral lessons rather than to detail particular historical events. Similarly, the Qurʾānic verses that deal with natural or scientific phenomena are meant to point out God's marvels in the universe rather than give exact explanation of these phenomena.[48]

Rashīd Riḍā begins his commentary on the story of Adam by conveying ʿAbduh's opinion that this narrative belongs to the category of the equivocal verses (*mutashābihāt*). This is a reference to Āl ʿImrān (3):7, which discusses two types of verses in the Qurʾān: unequivocal verses (*muḥkamāt*), constituting the essence of the book (*ummu al-kitāb*), and equivocal ones.[49] Āl ʿImrān (3):7 contrasts the attitude of those with sick hearts, who pursue these equivocal verses to cause dissention, with those who are established in knowledge and who submit and relegate exact meaning of these verses to God. Riḍā notes that the meaning of the verses dealing with the beginning of creation cannot be determined easily (*yaʿizzu al-wuqufu ʿalayhā*). According to ʿAbduh, these verses cannot be interpreted literally (*ʿalā ẓāhirihā*) if they lead to an understanding that contradicts sound belief in God or his angels.[50] God's incomparability (*tanzīh*) is the essence, or fundamental principle (*aṣl*), of Muslim creed. Muslims have developed two main methods to deal with verses that challenge this principle. The first is the method of the pious ancestors (*salaf*), according to which recourse must be made and priority must be given to the main textual references that emphasize God's incomparability, such as "There is nothing like Him" (al-Shūrāʾ [42]:11). Moreover, the matter should be relegated to God with submission and recognition of human inability to comprehend the fullness of God's words, which aim ultimately to convey ethical and moral values with examples and expressions that suit human understanding. The second is the method of the succeeding generations of the learned (*khalaf*), according to which the fundamental principles of Islam are based on sound reason. Any literal or apparent (*ẓāhir*) indication that constitutes categorical infringement to the dictates of sound reason should be interpreted in a manner that corresponds to these rationally compatible fundamental principles.[51] Both ʿAbduh and Riḍā state that they follow these two methods, although the latter is careful to indicate that, in reconciling the dictates of reason and revelation, he relies on the work of the later Ḥanbalī jurists Ibn Taymiyyah and Ibn al-Qayyim.[52]

Concerning the actions mentioned in al-Aʿrāf (7):11, Riḍā refers to the opinions al-Ṭabarī recorded but, following ʿAbduh, supports al-Rāzī's opinion on the interpretation of the word *khalq* as *taqdīr*, which emphasizes God's foreknowledge and control of His creation.[53] On the question of whether Iblīs belonged to the angels, Riḍā records the various views on the issue and concludes that the answer ultimately belongs to the domain of the unseen (*al-ghayb*), whose reality is dependent on definitive reports.[54] The command given to the angels to prostrate themselves before Adam is meant to denote honor and dignity, not worship.[55]

Concerning the dialogue between God and Iblīṣ in al-Aʿrāf (7):12–18, Riḍā records two types of interpretation that ʿAbduh gave for these verses. The first is in line with the literal or apparent meaning of the text, and the other is based on a metaphorical understanding of Iblīs and the angels. According to the first interpretation, the divine command given to Iblīs denotes obligation, and the dialogue mentioned in these verses represents an actual incident that took place somehow. According to this reading, Iblīs's sin involves several types of blatant errors, which are all based on his envious and insolent attitude. First, he objected to God's order when it did not match his preference and inclination. Second, he sought to support his attitude with an argument. Third, in rejecting the divine command, he elevated himself to a status equivalent to that of God. This in turn conflicts with the proper attitude of a servant of God, which should be marked by acceptance and submission. Fourth, he appealed to the substances from which he and Adam were created to prove his superiority. Fifth, he overlooked other important considerations, such as the creation of Adam by God's hands, the breathing of divine soul into Adam, and his endowment with knowledge and aptitude for learning.[56]

According to the metaphorical interpretation of these verses, the story is meant to give an illustration (*tamthīl*) of the universe's natural features and characteristics as well as the different human instincts. The angels stand for the spiritual forces (*al-quwā al-rawḥāniyya*) ingrained in each type of God's creation to help it fulfill its intended objective. Man is given the ability to use and manipulate these forces, which is indicated in these verses by the divine command for angels to prostrate themselves before Adam. This ability, however, denotes an ontological command of being (*amr takwīnī*). It is tied to the divine will and God's power to create by the mere command and without causes (Yā Sīn [36]:82). It describes the divine act of creation and the way it is constituted, which is different from the legislative command (*amr tashrīʿī/taklīfī*).[57] Similarly, Iblīs stands for a special type of evil force that works against the natural (beneficent) order and that man is exhorted to resist and subdue.[58] According to this interpretation, this passage, especially the dialogue between God and Iblīs, describes the existing reality of human and satanic characteristics (*bayān al-wāqiʿ min ṣifat ṭabīʿat al-bashar wa-ṭabīʿat al-shayṭān*) and the struggle between these different forces.[59]

Riḍā employs ʿAbduh's two approaches—the apparent and the metaphorical—to interpret the rest of the story. Concerning the garden, ʿAbduh addresses the question of its nature and reality: Is it the Garden of Eden or a different garden on Earth? ʿAbduh, following Abū Manṣūr al-Māturīdī, holds that the garden was on Earth; it was not the Garden of the Hereafter.[60] In the Qurʾān the word *janna* has also been used to refer to an earthly garden, as in al-Qalam (68):17.[61] Concerning the creation of Eve from Adam's rib, ʿAbduh notes that nothing in the Qurʾān supports this view. The other reference to Eve's creation in the ḥadīth does not have to be interpreted literally.[62] Iblīs's whispers are the evil thoughts or motivations, but like the majority of scholars, ʿAbduh argues that Iblīs may have actually appeared to Adam and his wife and spoken to them.[63]

According to a metaphorical interpretation, the garden is a state of bliss and happiness, Adam stands for humankind, and the forbidden tree is evil and disobedience.[64] This interpretation suggests that man's creation underwent several stages or phases (*aṭwār*). The first stage is childhood and naïveté and is marked by a lack of responsibilities or concerns. The command to dwell in paradise and enjoy its bounties is a metaphor for the reception of inspiration concerning good deeds and actions. Conversely, the inhibition to eat from the forbidden tree is a metaphor for reception of inspiration concerning evil deeds and actions. These two types of inspiration represent the second phase of human development: discernment (*tamyīz*). Iblīs's whispering represents the evil force that influences human nature and incites evil deeds, an aberration of the original good order of the human condition. Expulsion from paradise represents the difficulties and troubles that man experiences when he disturbs the innate balance of the human condition by committing sins. Adam's repentance stands for the realization, by sound human nature, of sin's consequences and the pursuit of divine forgiveness, the third stage of human development.

ʿAbduh uses this three-stage process to describe human development at the individual as well as the collective level. Each person can relate to this developmental process in his or her own life, and humanity at large has also passed through these three stages: simplicity and naïveté; discord and dissention, which is caused by people's conflicting interests; and reason and rationality, during which humanity seeks to achieve balance among the different conflicting interests. This last stage should lead to a final fourth stage representing completion and fulfillment of divine guidance, as is indicated in al-Baqara (2):38–39.[65] Riḍā comments on this metaphorical interpretation by emphasizing the need for divine guidance to achieve perfection and happiness. This developmental process cannot lead to ultimate perfection and happiness independent of divine guidance.[66]

In his commentary on the story of Adam in *Tafsīr al-Manār*, Riḍā juxtaposes these two modes of interpretation. In his discussion of the apparent mode, he follows the accepted interpretation of the story in the mainstream Sunnī tradition starting from al-Ṭabarī onward. In his discussion of the metaphorical mode, he records ʿAbduh's allegorical interpretation, which aims to provide a modern understanding of the text without the limitations of the inherited narrations and reports in the exegetical tradition.[67] Through this juxtaposition, Riḍā strives to appeal to two different audiences: those who are well versed in the Islamic tradition and familiar with classical exegetical works and readers with modern Western education who are reluctant to accept metaphysical explanations merely on the authority of premodern authors. For example, in his explanation of the interaction between humans and the invisible jinns and of their ability in inciting evil actions, Riḍā draws a parallel with the influence of invisible microbes and their ability to cause diseases.[68]

## Theological Implications

As noted previously, the Qurʾānic narrative about Adam has been used in various debates on a wide range of theological and metaphysical issues, such as the nature of Iblīs and his relationship to the angels, the status of prophets vis-à-vis the angels, the infallibility of the prophets, human freedom and destiny, and, most importantly, the status of sinners and the impact of sin on belief.

### *Nature of Iblīs*

On the question of whether Iblīs belonged to the angels, al-Rāzī refers to two opinions. The first, which he attributes to some theologians (*baʿḍ al-mutakallimīn*), especially from the Muʿtazilī school, is that Iblīs was not from the angels. The second, which he attributes to the jurists (*al-fuqahāʾ*), is that he was from the angels.[69] As noted previously, al-Rāzī gives the argument for each opinion without supporting either of them. For example, to support the first opinion, he writes that first, according to al-Kahf (18):50, Iblīs belonged to the jinn, which means that he was not from the angels. Second, Iblīs has progeny, whereas the angels do not. Third, the angels are infallible, whereas Iblīs is not. Fourth, Iblīs is created out of fire, whereas the angels are created out of light. Fifth, the angels are God's messengers, and God's messengers are infallible, which is not true of Iblīs. On the other hand, to support the second view, al-Rāzī writes that, first, the command was given to the angels, and Iblīs was among them. Second, Iblīs was mentioned as an exception; otherwise, he is considered one of the rest of the angels.[70]

### *The Prophets and the Angels*

The divine command to the angels to prostrate themselves before Adam triggered a debate about the superiority of Adam (the prophets) over the angels. Al-Rāzī gives an account of the debate between the Ash'arites and the Mu'tazilites on this issue. According to al-Rāzī, the majority of the former hold that Adam is superior to (*afḍal min*) the angels. The Mu'tazilites, on the other hand, argue that the angels are superior to the prophets. Al-Rāzī also notes that this latter view is the opinion of the Shī'is and also some Ash'arites, such as Abū Bakr al-Bāqillānī. Although al-Rāzī does not explicitly support either of these views, he concludes his discussion by recording the responses of the Mu'tazilites to the arguments of the Ash'arites, which may indirectly indicate that he believes that the angels are superior.[71]

A related point is the debate on the prophets' infallibility (*'iṣmah*) and protection from the commission of sins. Al-Rāzī divides his discussion of the prophets' infallibility into four sections: religious conviction (*i'tiqād*), transmission of the divine message (*tablīgh*), judgment on religious issues (*futyā*), and actions in general. With regard to religious conviction and belief, the majority of Muslims hold that the prophets cannot be accused of disbelief. Some Kharijites, however, allowed the possibility that the prophets could fall into disbelief as a result of commission of sins because, according to their view, this would amount to disbelief. With regard to transmission of the divine message, a consensus exists that prophets are protected from lying or forgery; otherwise, it would be difficult to trust their statements. While most scholars note that such lapses by prophets cannot occur either intentionally or unintentionally, some argue that this may occur only unintentionally, which is also the case for judgment on religious issues.

In the category of general actions, al-Rāzī records five main views. The first, which he attributes to the extreme literalists (*ḥashawiyyah*), holds that prophets can commit major sins intentionally. The second, which he attributes to the majority of Mu'tazilites, holds that prophets are protected from the commission of major sins but not minor sins, even intentionally, with the exception of certain abhorrent sins, such as lying or cheating in measurement. The third, which he attributes to al-Jubā'ī from the Mu'tazilites, holds that prophets cannot commit either major or minor sins intentionally but can commit them on the basis of understanding and interpretation (*ta'wīl*). The fourth, which he does not attribute to anyone, holds that prophets do not commit sins at all except unintentionally or by mistake. Unlike their followers, who should not be held responsible for unintentional sins, the prophets have stronger faith and more powerful self-control, and, therefore, they are held responsible even in these cases. The fifth view, which al-Rāzī attributes to the Shī'ites, holds that the prophets are protected from all types of sins whether they are committed intentionally or unintentionally.[72] The Shī'ites believe that the prophets are protected from the time of their birth. Most Mu'tazilites believe that they are protected from the time they reach puberty and that they are also protected from disbelief and major sins before prophethood.

Most Ash'arites as well as some Mu'tazilites believe prophets cannot commit sins after prophethood but may do so before they become prophets.[73]

Following the explanation of these views, al-Rāzī interprets Adam's sin on the grounds that, when Adam committed the sin, he was not a prophet. He became a prophet only afterward.[74] But even assuming that Adam committed the sin when he was already a prophet, al-Rāzī offers several justifications: that Adam committed the sin unintentionally, which is tenable; that he did it intentionally, which would be untenable, according to the Ash'arī view; that it was based on a wrong reasoning (*ijtihād*), according to most Mu'tazilites, which al-Rāzī does not agree with.[75]

## *Human Freedom*

The story of Adam was also invoked with regard to the important theological questions of human freedom, the scope of voluntary actions, and destiny. For example, in his commentary on al-A'rāf (7):16, al-Zamakhsharī criticizes the determinist attitude on human free will of the group he refers to as al-Mujabbirah (usually a term used by the Mu'tazilites to refer to their opponents, particularly the Ash'arites) and vindicates the Mu'tazilī view that God does only what is best for humans. The term *aghwaytanī* (seduced me) implies that God seduced Iblīs; the Ash'arites take this term literally since God is the creator of all actions, good and bad. Al-Zamakhsharī, however, following the Mu'tazilī attitude, vindicates the divine will by interpreting Iblīs's statement as "Because of my own transgression and fall into sin, I will seduce others."[76] This interpretation goes against mainstream Sunnism, which can be traced back to the early commentators, such as al-Ṭabarī, who chose a more literal interpretation that indicates God's control of the causes of all actions.[77] Similarly, al-Rāzī refers to Iblīs's refusal to obey the divine command. He starts by articulating the Mu'tazilī view that supports freedom of choice and refutes absolute determinism (*jabr*), a view he attributes to al-Qāḍī (most probably 'Abd al-Jabbār [d. 415/1024]).[78] Al-Rāzī writes that Iblīs expressed his refusal despite his ability to comply and obey the command. This is understood from the term *abā*, which means "refuse" or "decline" and denotes willful abstinence. If Iblīs did not have the ability to comply, his condemnation would not have made sense because responsibility goes with freedom and ends with lack thereof. Ultimately, according to this view, "whoever holds an opinion that would amount to the acquittal of Iblīs, it would be as if he has concluded a losing transaction" (*man i'taqada madhhab yuqīmu al-'udhra li-iblīs fa-huwa khāsir al-ṣafqah*).[79] Al-Rāzī responds to this classic Mu'tazilī view with a strong support of the Ash'arī voluntarist attitude relegating all power to God alone, who is omnipotent and omniscient and whose will is above questioning.[80]

As noted previously, in addition to this traditional interpretation of the scope of human freedom within the theological debates between the Ash'arites and the Mu'tazilites, Muḥammad 'Abduh argued for a metaphorical interpretation of the story of Adam and the dialogue between God and Iblīs. According to this interpretation, the story depicts the various forces in the universe and the human struggle with these forces.[81] This interpretation raises the theological question of evil and the significance of its existence in the universe. 'Abduh argues that the meaning of evil is relative (*amr i'tibārī*) and depends on both the immediate and the ultimate consequences of what is perceived to be evil. For example, painful or harmful actions can result in useful and beneficial consequences, both in this life and in the hereafter.[82]

The story of Adam raises questions not only about the existence of evil but also about existence per se and the wisdom behind the creation of the universe. On this topic 'Abduh notes that the ultimate divine wisdom in creation can be pursued by exploring the attributes of divine perfection as manifested in His design and actions so that He may be known, worshipped, praised, glorified, and thanked.[83] Divine wisdom also entails the creation of what we know and what we do not know in a certain order with specific characteristics and their opposites. In the interaction between opposites, both within man and in interhuman interaction, the various divine attributes are manifested, and His wisdom is realized. The story of Adam and Iblīs is told in order to demonstrate both the capacity to sin and ways of overcoming sin's consequences. It also gives examples of proper and improper attitudes on the part of competent servants (*mukallafīn*) in the eternal struggle between the descendants of Adam and Iblīs.[84]

### *Sin and Belief*

The most important theological question involving the issue of sin, however, is sin's consequences for one's state of belief and standing as a believer. This has been one of the polarizing questions in Islamic theology. For example, in al-Baqara (2):34, Iblīs is described as being a disbeliever (as a result of his refusal to obey the command). This in turn raised a question about the occurrence of disbelief after belief; is this state of disbelief emergent, or has it always been there despite claims of belief? Al-Rāzī records two views. According to the first, if disbelief occurs after belief, this means that the original belief was not sincere. The Mu'tazilites describe the original state of belief as hypocrisy (*nifāq*) because it ended up leading to disbelief. Others describe the original state of belief using the theory of ultimate consequence (*muwāfāh*). According to this theory, what matters is the final state in which one ends his life (*khatm*). If one ends his life in a state of belief, his prior claim of belief must have been sincere and vice versa. Because Iblīs committed disbelief, this means that he had never been a (sincere) believer. According to the second view, disbelief can occur after belief, and this is what happened with Iblīs.[85]

The question of the impact of sin, particularly major sin, on belief has not only inspired heated theological debates but has also been one of the main factors that determined the boundaries among the various theological schools. For example, a famous anecdote depicts the emergence of the Muʿtazilī school after a disagreement between its founder, Wāṣil ibn ʿAṭāʾ (d. 181/797), and his teacher, al-Ḥasan al-Baṣrī, on the status of the grave sinner. According to mainstream Sunnism, a grave sinner remains a believer even though sinfulness (*fusūq*) detracts from the state of pure belief. The Kharijites held the view that the commission of a major sin amounts to disbelief. Wāṣil's view was that sinfulness constitutes a position between belief and disbelief (*manizilah bayna al-manzilatayn*).[86] Other accounts of the emergence of the Muʿtazilites exist, but this principle became one of the five cardinal principles of Muʿtazilism.[87] The Kharijites found support for their opinion in al-Baqara (2):34 on the grounds that Iblīs was described as a disbeliever because of his sin. Al-Rāzī, however, responds by emphasizing that this view is not tenable on two grounds. First, for those who believe in an original or latent state of disbelief, this argument is not warranted since in this case Iblīs was a disbeliever from the beginning. Second, for those who do not believe in an original state of disbelief, Iblīs is described as a disbeliever mainly because of his arrogance and insolence—as confirmed by his statement, "I am better than him"—which is different from a normal or regular sin.[88]

## Sin, *Nafs*, and *Ẓulm al-Nafs*

Some of the important issues for any discussion of sin include its causes, motivations, and consequences. As noted previously, several theological questions have been raised concerning the range and scope of human will in the occurrence or commission of sin, on the one hand, and the impact of sin on one's belief and standing as a believer, on the other. Another important element in this context is the role of one's (lower) self (*nafs*) in the commission of sin. Other related questions are, What is the nature and reality of this *nafs*? How is it attached to the body? What is its relationship to the spirit (*rūḥ*)? and Are they two separate entities? Related terms include heart (*qalb*) and intellect (*ʿaql*). Abū Ḥāmid al-Ghazālī notes that these four terms (*qalb*, *nafs*, *rūḥ*, and *ʿaql*) are often confused as they tend to be used interchangeably. He explains that while each of them has a unique definition and independent reality, they also share one common dimension, which is the source of the confusion. From al-Ghazālī's spiritual perspective, the central term and concept is the heart. This understanding is based on the prophetic report predicating overall well-being on the state and condition of one's heart.[89] According to al-Ghazālī, each of these terms has two meanings, and while they differ with regard to the first meaning, they all share in the second.

The first meaning of the heart is the physical organ located in the left side of one's chest. The second meaning refers to a divine, spiritual, delicate entity associated with the bodily heart (*laṭīfah rabbāniyyah rawḥāniyyah lahā bi-hādhā al-qalb al-jismānī taʿalluq*). This entity constitutes the sum total of human cognitive as well as spiritual powers. The exact association between this heart and the physical one is unknown, like the attachment between the body and the spirit. The first meaning of the spirit (*rūḥ*) refers to a delicate entity (*jism laṭīf*) that originates in the cavity of the physical heart and spreads throughout the human body like a light beam flowing over the different parts of a house. The second meaning of the spirit, mentioned in al-Isrāʾ (17):85, refers to the cognitive and spiritual powers mentioned previously. The first meaning of self (*nafs*) is the sum total of the powers of anger and lust in man; it is the essence of all detestable and blameworthy characteristics. This is the meaning intended when one talks about combating one's (lower) self and subduing it (*mujāhadat al-nafs wa-kasruhā*). The second meaning of the self, like that of *qalb* and *rūḥ*, refers to the human cognitive and spiritual powers associated with the heart and the spirit. Ibn al-Qayyim notes that the term *nafs* is also used in the Qurʾān to refer to the whole person (*al-dhāt bi-jumlatihāh*), as in Yūsuf (16):111 and Muddathir (74):38.[90] This usage is closer to al-Ghazālī's second definition. The first meaning of intellect (*ʿaql*) is knowledge of the reality of things (*al-ʿilm bi-ḥaqāʾiq al-umūr*), and in this sense the word refers to the type or quality of knowledge. The second meaning refers to the discerning power that is associated with the common definition mentioned previously for the heart, spirit, and self.[91]

The association between *nafs* and sin is usually made with reference to the first meaning, highlighting the influence of anger and lust. The self in this sense is considered one of the main driving forces toward sin. Ironically, self in this capacity is considered one's own worst enemy. Maturity and overall well-being, both material and spiritual, are measured by one's ability to control and tame this egoistic self. In the Qurʾān this definition of *nafs* is referred to as the one commanding evil (*ammārah bil-sūʾ*), as in Yūsuf (12):18 and 53. Both verses relate to the story of Prophet Yūsuf (Joseph). The first is the response of Yūsuf's father to what his other children said about Yūsuf's being devoured by the wolf. Yūsuf's father thought his children were not telling the truth and that they must have plotted against Yūsuf. He describes their evil action as being driven by their (lower) selves (*sawwalat lakum anfusukum amran*). Similarly in verse 53, the self is blamed as a force that incites sin.

In addition to this negative aspect of the self, the Qur'ān refers to benign characteristics of the self, describing it in al-Fajr (89):27 as reassured or righteous (*muṭma'innah*) and in al-Qiyāma (75):2 as self-reproaching (*lawwāmah*). Al-Rāzī refers to a disagreement about whether there is one or multiple selves in light of these different descriptions in the Qur'ān. He concludes that the verified opinion is that there is one *nafs* that could have different characteristics depending on its inclination and disposition (*al-nafs al-insāniyyah shay' wāḥid wa-lahā ṣifāt kathīrah*). If it turns toward the divine realm, the self becomes righteous, but if it turns toward anger and lust, it commands evil.[92] Al-Ghazālī associates the latter self with the first meaning of *nafs* (connected with anger and lust) and the other two (*muṭma'innah* and *lawwāmah*) with the second meaning, related to the sum total of human cognitive and spiritual powers.

In addition to describing the (lower) self as a driving force toward sin, the Qur'ān describes sin's effect on the (overall) self. In this context sin is considered a type of injustice, transgression, or wrong against one's own self or being (*ẓulm al-nafs*). This is a common expression in the Qur'ān and is used in the story of Adam in al-Baqara (2):35, in which the act of disobedience is described as a form of *ẓulm*.[93] In al-A'rāf (7):23, as Adam and his wife asked for forgiveness, they acknowledged that they had wronged their own selves through the act of disobedience. The expression was similarly used in al-A'rāf (7):177. The association between sin and *ẓulm al-nafs* is rooted in the negative consequences to the self of sin in the form of either forfeiture of reward or incurrence of punishment, whether in this world or the next.[94] A survey of the contexts in which this expression occurs in the Qur'ān reveals that it is almost always associated with sin and the act of sinning.[95]

## Conclusion

The concept of sin in the Qur'ān is defined and characterized by the notion of disobedience in the broadest sense. It is associated with a number of terms that convey a number of meanings, including error, wrong, bad deed, guilt, infraction, and crime. The story of Adam and Eve and their encounter with Iblīs exemplifies the Qur'ānic concept of sin and also the (im)proper attitude of a sinner. Adam and Eve were forgiven after they had acknowledged their wrongdoing, but Iblīs was damned because of his arrogance and insolence.

The story offers an instructive illustrative example of the various methodological approaches that have been employed in the extended exegetical tradition. Whereas al-Ṭabarī relied on received reports and sought to verify the most reliable ones among them, al-Rāzī relied on various other resources that became available by the time he compiled his work in the seventh/thirteenth century, particularly in the theological tradition. In the modern period, Rashīd Riḍā, following his teacher Muḥammad ʿAbduh, sought to offer an interpretation that took the modern context into consideration. By offering two parallel interpretations, one literal and another metaphorical, ʿAbduh and Riḍā aimed to appeal to both those who are familiar with the Islamic exegetical tradition and those who find it difficult to rely exclusively on metaphysical arguments. The story of Adam raised several important theological questions ranging from anthropomorphism to human destiny and freedom of action. The impact of sin on one's belief and on one's standing as a believer remained a polarizing concept in Islamic theology with repercussions continuing to the present day, especially among militant groups.

While the Qur'ān points out the role of the (lower) self as one of the main causes of sin, it also notes the impact of sin on one's (overall) self, as is evident in the frequent use of the expression "wronging one's self or soul" (*ẓulm al-nafs*) to describe various types of disobedience. Through sin one harms oneself by forfeiting the chance of being rewarded for either obedience or avoidance of disobedience, on the one hand, or, on the other, by subjecting oneself to punishment in this world or the next as a result of disobedience. Finally, the story of Adam teaches that the struggle against sin is part of the eternal battle of the children of Adam against Iblīs and his followers.

## Notes

1 The term *maʿṣiya* itself is mentioned in the Qur'ān twice in al-Mujādala (58):8–9. A synonymous verbal noun (*ʿiṣyān*) is mentioned in 49:7. Additionally, various derivatives in different verb forms are used about thirty times. See Muḥammad Fu'ād ʿAbd al-Bāqī, *al-Muʿjam al-Mufahras li-Alfāẓ al-Qu'ān al-Karīm* (Beirut: Mu'assassat al-Aʿlamī lil-Maṭbūʿāt, 1999), 465–66.

2 The term *khaṭī'a* is mentioned ten times in both singular and plural forms. See ibid., 241. The term *ithm* is mentioned thirty-five times. See ibid., 19. The term *dhanb* is used thirty-eight times in different singular and plural forms. See ibid., 280–81. The term *sayyi'a* is mentioned about fifty-seven times in different forms. See ibid., 373–74.

3 See ibid., 432–33.

4 For a starting point on this issue in English, see W. R. W. Gardner, *The Qur'anic Doctrine of Sin* (Madras: Christian Literature Society, 1914), in which the author analyzes the various terms associated with the concept of sin in the Qur'ān and explores the relationship between sin and other notions, such as transgression, prohibition, injustice, and oppression.

5 Abū Jaʿfar Muḥammad ibn Jarīr al-Ṭabarī, *Jāmiʿ al-Bayān ʿan Ta'wīl Āy al-Qur'ān* (Cairo: Muṣtafā al-Bābī al-Ḥalabī, 1968), 5:37.

6 Ibid., 40.

7 Ibid., 38. See, for example, Qur'ān 6:151–52; 17:23–38; 25:68.

8 Ibid., 39.

9 Ibid., 41.

10 Ibid., 38; see also Abū ʿAbd Allāh Muḥammad ibn Aḥmad al-Qurṭubī, *al-Jāmiʿ li-Aḥkām al-Qurʾān*, ed. Muḥāmmad Ibrāhīm al-Ḥifnāwī and Maḥmūd Ḥamid ʿUthmān (Cairo: Dār al-Ḥadīth, 1996), 5:162–66.

11 The story of Adam is mentioned in the Qurʾān in seven places: 2:30–38, 7:11–27, 15:26–42, 17:61–63, 18:50, 20:15–23, and 38:71–85. See Fakhr al-Dīn Muḥammad ibn ʿUmar al-Rāzī, *al-Tafsīr al-Kabīr* (Beirut: Dār Iḥyāʾ al-Turāth, 1990), 14:29.

12 Abdullah Yūsuf ʿAlī, *The Meaning of the Holy Qurʾān* (Beltsville, MD: Amana Publications, 1989), 25.

13 Muḥammad Husayn al-Dhahabī, *al-Tafsīr wa-al-Mufassirūn* (Cairo: Dār al-Kutub al-Ḥadīthah, 1976), 1:167.

14 For a discussion of ibn Ḥanbal on this matter, see ibid., 47. Ibn Ḥajar al-ʿAsqalānī adds to these three reports concerning virtues or specific merits, *faḍāʾil* (e.g., of specific sūra, types of food, or people). See Aḥmad ibn ʿAlī Ibn Ḥajar al-ʿAsqalānī, *Lisān al-Mizān* (Beirut: Dār Iḥyāʾ al-Turāth al-ʿArabī, 1995), 1:20. For an example that shows the range of reports that have developed around the Qurʾānic story of Adam in the Islamic literary tradition, see M. J. Kister, "Legends in *tafsīr* and *Ḥadīth* Literature: The Creation of Adam and Related Stories," in *Approaches to the History of Interpretation of the Qurʾān*, ed. Andrew Rippin (Oxford: Oxford University Press, 1988), 82–114. After a survey of related reports, Kister notes, "The material discussed . . . add up to no more than a drop in the sea when compared to the totality of the lore transmitted about Adam in Islamic sources." See ibid., 114.

15 The most famous introductory survey in the West remains Ignaz Goldziher's *Die Richtungen der islamischen Koranauslegun*, which was published in 1920. It was also published in English as *Schools of Koranic Commentators*, trans. Wolfgang H. Behn (Wiesbaden: Harrassowitz Verlag, 2006). The most famous survey in Arabic in the modern period is al-Dhahabī's *al-Tafsīr wa-al-Mufassirūn*. Goldziher's work has been translated into Arabic twice (the first effort was an incomplete translation), and al-Dhahabī takes note of it. On the reception of Goldziher's work in the Arab world, see Walid Saleh, "al-Tarjamah al-Arabiyyah li-Kitāb Ignaz Goldziher 'al-Madhāhb al-Islāmiyyah fī Tafsīr al-Qurʾān' wa-Atharuhā fī al-Dirāsāt al-Islāmiyyah: Qirā'ah Ulā,'" *Journal of Qurʾanic Studies* 14, no. 1 (2012): 201–14.

16 EI$^2$, s.v. Tafsīr (A. Rippin).

17 Al-Dhahabī, *al-Tafsīr wa-al-Mufassirūn*, 1:152, 204, 255, 288.

18 Although al-Ṭabarī's work is usually referred to as an example of a report-based *tafsīr*, some researchers consider it a work that combines both approaches (*riwāyah* and *dirāyah*), especially in light of the opinion that authentic and reliable prophetic reports on *tafsīr* are not numerous. See, for example, ʿAbd Allāh Maḥmūd Shiḥātah's study on the *tafsīr* of Muqātil ibn Sulaymān, which is considered the first complete commentary on the Qurʾān. See Muqātil ibn Sulaymān, *Tafsīr Muqātil ibn Sulaymān*, ed. ʿAbd Allāh Maḥmūd Shiḥātah (Cairo: al-Ḥayʾah al-Miṣriyyah al-ʿAmmah lil-Kitāb, 1979), 5:16, 69.

19 Muḥammad Rashīd Riḍā, *Tafsīr al-Qurʾān al-Ḥakīm al-Mashhūr bi-Tafsīr al-Manār*, 12 vols. (Beirut: Dār al-Kutub al-ʿIlmiyyah, 1999).

20 Jane Dammen McAuliff, "Quranic Hermeneutics: The Views of al-Ṭabarī and Ibn Kathīr," in Rippin, *Approaches to the History*, 48.

21 See, for example, Mahmoud Ayoub, *The Qur'ān and Its Interpreters* (New York: State University of New York, 1984), 1:71–93. Ayoub draws on a larger collection of *tafsīr* works in his account of the story of Adam in Sūrat al-Baqara. Ayoub, however, does not include *Tafsīr al-Manār*.

22 In some versions of al-Ṭabarī's manuscript, in this report the group to which Iblīs belonged is identified as *al-hinn* rather than *al-jinn*. In most *tafsīr* works, the term *jinn* is used to describe both the regular jinn and the group of the angels to which Iblīs belonged according to this report. The report makes the distinction between the two groups in terms of the substance from which each of them was created. Although both are created out of fire, the report refers to different verses in the Qur'ān that describe the creation of jinn. According to the report, Iblīs's group is created out of (*samūm*), which is mentioned in 15:27, and the regular jinn are created out of (*mārij min nār*), which is mentioned in 55:15. Ayoub uses the term *ḥinn* to refer to Iblīs's group.

23 Al-Ṭabarī, *Jāmi' al-Bayān*,1:201; and Ayoub, *Qur'ān and Its Interpreters*, 74.

24 Al-Ṭabarī, *Jāmi' al-Bayān*,1:202.

25 Ibid., 203.

26 Al-Rāzī refers to these two views—i.e., whether God's discourse was addressed to all the angels or only to the group to which Iblīs belonged. He chose the former view because the term used, *al-malā'ika* (angels), does not indicate any specification. See al-Rāzī, *al-Tafsīr al-Kabīr*, 2:165.

27 Al-Ṭabarī, *Jāmi' al-Bayān*,1:203.

28 Ibid., 205.

29 Ibid., 206. On this point Mahmoud Ayoub observes, "It may be argued that the purpose of the entire drama of creation was for God to manifest His knowledge and power and to expose the pride of Iblis." Ayoub, *Qur'ān and Its Interpreters*, 75.

30 Al-Ṭabarī, *Jāmi' al-Bayān*,1:229.

31 Ibid.

32 Ibid., 233; see also al-Rāzī, *al-Tafsīr al-Kabīr*, 3:5.

33 Al-Ṭabarī, *Jāmi' al-Bayān*,1:235–37.

34 Ibid., 238–39.

35 Ibid., 8:152–53.

36 Ibid., 144.

37 Ibid., 146.

38 Ibid., 127.

39 Al-Rāzī, *al-Tafsīr al-Kabīr*, 14:29–30

40 Ibid., 2:212.

41 Ibid., 2:212–23, 14:30.

42 Ibid., 2:213, 14:31.

43 Ibid., 14:35.

44 Ibid., 3:4. See also ibid., 14:35, 44.

45 Ibid., 3:5.

46 Ibid., 14:46.

47 Ibid., 3:16.

48 Riḍā, *Tafsīr al-Manār*, 1:177, 231.

49 For a discussion of this verse in light of the interpretations given by al-Ṭabarī and Ibn Kathīr, see McAuliff, "Quranic Hermeneutics," 51–62.

50 Riḍā, *Tafsīr al-Manār*, 1:209.

51 Ibid., 209–10.

52 Ibid., 210.

53 Ibid., 8:290.

54 Ibid., 1:220.

55 Ibid., 8:291.

56 Ibid., 291–93.

57 Ibid., 1:232, 8:300.

58 Ibid., 1:222–27.

59 Ibid., 8:300.

60 Ibid., 1: 228–29, 8:305–6.

61 Ibid., 8:305.

62 Ibid., 1:232, 8:306. He gives another example in 21:37, which indicates that man is a creature (created out) of haste.

63 Ibid., 8:307.

64 Ibid., 1:233; 8:307.

65 Ibid., 1:233–35.

66 Ibid., 1:235, 8:307

67 Ibid., 8:312–13.

68 Ibid., 322, 313. Similarly, in his interpretation of 2:275, ʿAbduh draws a parallel between the influence of jinn and the influence of microbes, which he argues can be considered a type of jinn. See ibid., 3:81. On this aspect of *Tafsīr al-Manār* and ʿAbduh's attempt to reconcile the Qurʾān and modern science, see Goldziher, *Schools of Koranic Commentators*, 224.

69 Al-Rāzī, *al-Tafsīr al-Kabīr*, 2:213.

70 Ibid., 214–15.

71 Ibid., 215–35.

72 Ibid., 3:7.

73 Ibid., 7–8.

74 See also the reiteration of this view concerning 7:25. Ibid., 14:50.

75 Ibid., 3:12–15. The *ijtihād* that the Muʿtazilites refer to here concerns whether the inhibition covered the genus of the forbidden tree or only an individual tree.

76 Al-Zamakhsharī, *al-Kashshāf ʿan ḥaqāʾīq ghawamiḍ al-tanzīl wa-ʿuyūn al-aqāwīl fī wujūh al-taʾwīl*, ed. ʿĀdil Aḥmad ʿAbd al-Mawjūd and ʿAlī Muḥammad Muʿawwaḍ (Riyadh: Maktabat al-ʿubaykn, 1998), 2:466.

77 Al-Ṭabarī, *Jāmiʿ al-Bayān*, 8:133–34.

78 He referred to him by name in his interpretation of 2:37. Al-Rāzī, *al-Tafsīr al-Kabīr*, 3:21.

79 Ibid., 2:235.

80 Ibid. The same argument is used with reference to 7:16. See ibid., 14:37–39. In the Ashʿarī school it is asserted that the Muʿtazilī view on the divine obligation to do what is best (*riʿāyat al-aṣlaḥ*) was one of the main factors that caused the conversion of the founder of Ashʿarism, Abū al-Ḥasan al-Ashʿarī, from Muʿtazilism. This is usually traced to a debate between Abū al-Ḥasan al-Ashʿarī and his teacher, Abū ʿAlī al-Jubāʾī, on the fate of three individuals: a believer, a disbeliever, and a child. See Tāj al-Dīn ʿAbd al-Wahhāb ibn ʿAlī ibn ʿAbd al-Kāfī al-Subkī, *Ṭabaqāt al-Shāfiʿiyyah al-Kubrā*, ed. Maḥmūd Muḥammad al-Ṭanāḥī and ʿAbd al-Fattāḥ al-Ḥilw (Cairo: Dār Iḥyāʾ al-Kutub al-ʿArabiyyah, 1990) 3:356. See also Fazlur Rahman, *Islam,* 2nd ed. (Chicago: University of Chicago Press, 1979), 91.

81 Riḍā, *Tafsīr al-Manār*, 8:300.

82 Ibid., 301. He gives the example of a painful medication that is used to achieve recovery. Similarly, sacrificing (personal) wealth for public causes can be another example of how loss, in a sense, at the personal level can result in gain, in a sense, at the collective level.

83 Ibid.

84 Ibid., 302–3.

85 Al-Rāzī, *al-Tafsīr al-Kabīr*, 2:236–37.

86 Shams al-Dīn Aḥmad ibn Muḥammad ibn Abī Bakr ibn Khallikan, *Wafayāt al-Aʿyān wa-Anbāʾ Abnāʾ al-Zamān*, ed. Iḥsān ʿAbbās (Beirut: Dār Ṣādir, 1978), 6:8.

87 For a review of the different reports on the emergence of Muʿtazilism, see W. Montgomery Watt, *The Formative Period of Islamic Thought* (Oxford: One World Publications, 1998), 209–17.

88 Al-Rāzī, *al-Tafsīr al-Kabīr*, 2:238.

89 Aḥmad ibn ʿAlī Ibn Ḥajar al-ʿAsqalānī, *Fatḥ al-Bārī bi-Sharḥ Ṣaḥīḥ al-Bukhārī*, ed. ʿAbd al-ʿAzīz ibn ʿAbd Allāh ibn Bāz, Muḥammad Fuʾād ʿAbd al-Bāqī, and Muḥibb al-Dīn al-Khaṭīb (Beirut: Dār al-Maʿrifah, 1970), 1:126 (ch. *al-Īmān*, no. 52); and Abū Zakariyyā Muḥyī al-Dīn ibn Sharaf al-Nawawī, *Ṣaḥīḥ Muslim bi-Sharḥ al-Nawawī* (Cairo: al-Maṭbaʿah al-Miṣriyyah, 1929), 11:27 (ch. *al-Musāqāh wa-al-Muzāraʿah*).

90 Shams al-Dīn Muḥammad ibn Abī Bakr Ibn al-Qayyim, *al-Rūḥ* (Cairo: Dār al-Bayān al-ʿArabī, 1979), 348.

91 Abū Ḥāmid Muḥammad ibn Muḥammad al-Ghazālī, *Iḥyāʾ ʿUlūm al-Dīn* (Beirut: al-Maktabah al-ʿAṣriyyah, 1996), 3:5–6. See also Fakh al-Dīn al-Rāzī, *Kitāb al-Nafs wa-al-Rūḥ wa-Sharḥ Quwāhumā fī ʿIlm al-Akhlāq*, ed. ʿAbd Allāh Muḥammad ʿAbd Allāh Ismāʿīl (Cairo: al-Maktabah al-Azhariyyah lil-Turāth, 2013), 179.

92 Al-Rāzī, *Kitāb al-Nafs*, 157.

93 Yūsuf ʿAlī notes that *ẓulm* "implies harm, wrong, injustice, or transgression, and it may have reference to oneself; when the wrong is done to others it implies tyranny and oppression." See ʿAlī, *Meaning of the Holy Qurʾān*, 25. For more on the concept of *ẓulm al-nafs*, see George Hourani, *Reason and Tradition in Islamic Ethics* (Cambridge: Cambridge University Press, 1985), 49–56.

94 Al-Rāzī, *al-Tafsīr al-Kabīr*, 3:6 (with reference to 2:35); al-Ṭabarī, *Jāmiʿ al-Bayān*, 2:482 (with reference to 2:231).

95 ʿAbd al-Bāqī, *al-Muʿjam*, 436–40.

# Scripture Dialogues on Sin

**AT THE CORE** of every Building Bridges seminar is the commitment to spend substantial periods in small-group dialogue on preassigned texts. The 2014 seminar schedule provided for nine such sessions. This chapter provides the texts for each of the three dialogical sessions devoted to the topic of sin. The New Revised Standard Version is used for translations of all Bible passages. Abdullah Yusuf Ali's translation is used for the Qur'ān passages in Dialogues 2 and 3.

## DIALOGUE 1

### *Romans 5:11–21*

[11]But more than that, we even boast in God through our Lord Jesus Christ,
through whom we have now received reconciliation.
[12]Therefore, just as sin came into the world through one man, and death came
through sin, and so death spread to all because all have sinned—[13]sin was indeed
in the world before the law, but sin is not reckoned when there is no law. [14]Yet
death exercised dominion from Adam to Moses, even over those whose sins were
not like the transgression of Adam, who is a type of the one who was to come.
[15]But the free gift is not like the trespass. For if the many died through the one
man's trespass, much more surely have the grace of God and the free gift in the
grace of the one man, Jesus Christ, abounded for the many. [16]And the free gift is
not like the effect of the one man's sin. For the judgment following one trespass
brought condemnation, but the free gift following many trespasses brings justification. [17]If, because of the one man's trespass, death exercised dominion through
that one, much more surely will those who receive the abundance of grace and

the free gift of righteousness exercise dominion in life through the one man,
Jesus Christ.
[18]Therefore just as one man's trespass led to condemnation for all, so one
man's act of righteousness leads to justification and life for all. [19]For just as by the
one man's disobedience the many were made sinners, so by the one man's obedience the many will be made righteous. [20]But law came in, with the result that the
trespass multiplied; but where sin increased, grace abounded all the more, [21]so
that, just as sin exercised dominion in death, so grace might also exercise dominion through justification leading to eternal life through Jesus Christ our Lord.

▲ ▲ ▲

## *Genesis 3:1–24*

[1]Now the serpent was more crafty than any other wild animal that the Lord God
had made. He said to the woman, "Did God say, 'You shall not eat from any tree
in the garden'?" [2]The woman said to the serpent, "We may eat of the fruit of the
trees in the garden; [3]but God said, 'You shall not eat of the fruit of the tree that is
in the middle of the garden, nor shall you touch it, or you shall die.'" [4]But the
serpent said to the woman, "You will not die; [5]for God knows that when you eat
of it your eyes will be opened, and you will be like God, knowing good and evil."
[6]So when the woman saw that the tree was good for food, and that it was a delight
to the eyes, and that the tree was to be desired to make one wise, she took of its
fruit and ate; and she also gave some to her husband, who was with her, and he
ate. [7]Then the eyes of both were opened, and they knew that they were naked;
and they sewed fig leaves together and made loincloths for themselves.
[8]They heard the sound of the Lord God walking in the garden at the time of
the evening breeze, and the man and his wife hid themselves from the presence
of the Lord God among the trees of the garden. [9]But the Lord God called to the
man, and said to him, "Where are you?" [10]He said, "I heard the sound of you in
the garden, and I was afraid, because I was naked; and I hid myself." [11]He said,
"Who told you that you were naked? Have you eaten from the tree of which I
commanded you not to eat?" [12]The man said, "The woman whom you gave to be
with me, she gave me fruit from the tree, and I ate." [13]Then the Lord God said to
the woman, "What is this that you have done?" The woman said, "The serpent
tricked me, and I ate." [14]The Lord God said to the serpent,

"Because you have done this,
  cursed are you among all animals
  and among all wild creatures;

upon your belly you shall go,
and dust you shall eat
all the days of your life.
[15]I will put enmity between you and the woman,
and between your offspring and hers;
he will strike your head,
and you will strike his heel."

[16]To the woman he said,

"I will greatly increase your pangs in childbearing;
in pain you shall bring forth children,
yet your desire shall be for your husband,
and he shall rule over you."

[17]And to the man he said,

"Because you have listened to the voice of your wife,
and have eaten of the tree
about which I commanded you,
'You shall not eat of it,'
cursed is the ground because of you;
in toil you shall eat of it all the days of your life;
[18]thorns and thistles it shall bring forth for you;
and you shall eat the plants of the field.
[19]By the sweat of your face
you shall eat bread
until you return to the ground,
for out of it you were taken;
you are dust,
and to dust you shall return."

[20]The man named his wife Eve, because she was the mother of all who live. [21]And
the Lord God made garments of skins for the man and for his wife, and clothed
them.

[22]Then the Lord God said, "See, the man has become like one of us, knowing
good and evil; and now, he might reach out his hand and take also from the tree
of life, and eat, and live forever"—[23]therefore the Lord God sent him forth from
the garden of Eden, to till the ground from which he was taken. [24]He drove out

the man; and at the east of the garden of Eden he placed the cherubim, and a sword flaming and turning to guard the way to the tree of life.

## DIALOGUE 2

### *Al-A'rāf (7):10–27*

10 It is We Who have placed you with authority on earth, and provided you therein
with means for the fulfilment of your life: small are the thanks that ye give!
11 It is We Who created you and gave you shape; then We bade the angels bow
down to Adam, and they bowed down; not so Iblis; He refused to be of those who
bow down.
12 God said: "What prevented thee from bowing down when I commanded thee?"
He said: "I am better than he: Thou didst create me from fire, and him from clay."
13 God said: "Get thee down from this: it is not for thee to be arrogant here: get
out, for thou art of the meanest (of creatures)."
14 He said: "Give me respite till the day they are raised up."
15 God said: "Be thou among those who have respite."
16 He said: "Because thou hast thrown me out of the way, lo! I will lie in wait
for them on thy straight way:
17 "Then will I assault them from before them and behind them, from their right
and their left: Nor wilt thou find, in most of them, gratitude (for thy mercies)."
18 God said: "Get out from this, disgraced and expelled. If any of them follow
thee,—Hell will I fill with you all. 19 O Adam! dwell thou and thy wife in the
Garden, and enjoy (its good things) as ye wish: but approach not this tree, or ye
run into harm and transgression."
20 Then began Satan to whisper suggestions to them, bringing openly before
their minds all their shame that was hidden from them (before): he said: "Your
Lord only forbade you this tree, lest ye should become angels or such beings as
live forever." 21 And he swore to them both, that he was their sincere adviser.
22 So by deceit he brought about their fall: when they tasted of the tree, their
shame became manifest to them, and they began to sew together the leaves of the
garden over their bodies. And their Lord called unto them: "Did I not forbid you
that tree, and tell you that Satan was an avowed enemy unto you?"
23 They said: "Our Lord! We have wronged our own souls: If thou forgive us
not and bestow not upon us Thy Mercy, we shall certainly be lost."
24 God said: "Get ye down. With enmity between yourselves. On earth will be
your dwelling-place and your means of livelihood,—for a time." 25 He said: "Therein
shall ye live, and therein shall ye die; but from it shall ye be taken out (at last)."

[26]O ye Children of Adam! We have bestowed raiment upon you to cover your shame, as well as to be an adornment to you. But the raiment of righteousness,—that is the best. Such are among the Signs of Allah, that they may receive admonition!

[27]O ye Children of Adam! Let not Satan seduce you, in the same manner as He got your parents out of the Garden, stripping them of their raiment, to expose their shame: for he and his tribe watch you from a position where ye cannot see them: We made the evil ones friends (only) to those without faith.

## DIALOGUE 3

### *Romans 7:14–25*

[14]For we know that the law is spiritual; but I am of the flesh, sold into slavery
under sin. [15]I do not understand my own actions. For I do not do what I want, but
I do the very thing I hate. [16]Now if I do what I do not want, I agree that the law is
good. [17]But in fact it is no longer I that do it, but sin that dwells within me. [18]For
I know that nothing good dwells within me, that is, in my flesh. I can will what is
right, but I cannot do it. [19]For I do not do the good I want, but the evil I do not
want is what I do. [20]Now if I do what I do not want, it is no longer I that do it, but
sin that dwells within me.

[21]So I find it to be a law that when I want to do what is good, evil lies close at
hand. [22]For I delight in the law of God in my inmost self, [23]but I see in my members another law at war with the law of my mind, making me captive to the law
of sin that dwells in my members. [24]Wretched man that I am! Who will rescue me
from this body of death? [25]Thanks be to God through Jesus Christ our Lord!

So then, with my mind I am a slave to the law of God, but with my flesh I am a slave to the law of sin.

### *Al-Aʿrāf (7):177–79*

[177]Evil as an example are people who reject Our signs and wrong their own souls.

[178]Whom God doth guide,—he is on the right path: whom He rejects from His guidance,—such are the persons who perish.

[179]Many are the Jinns and men we have made for Hell: They have hearts wherewith they understand not, eyes wherewith they see not, and ears wherewith they hear not. They are like cattle,—nay more misguided: for they are heedless (of warning).

▲ ▲ ▲

### *Yūsuf (12):18*

18They stained his shirt with false blood. He said: "Nay, but your minds have made up a tale (that may pass) with you, (for me) patience is most fitting: Against that which ye assert, it is God (alone) Whose help can be sought."

▲ ▲ ▲

### *Yūsuf (12):53*

53"Nor do I absolve my own self (of blame): the (human) soul is certainly prone to evil, unless my Lord do bestow His Mercy: but surely my Lord is Oft-forgiving, Most Merciful."

# PART III

# Forgiveness

# Forgiveness and Redemption in Christian Understanding

SUSAN EASTMAN

***FORGIVENESS* AND *REDEMPTION*** are two related terms that highlight interlocking views of the human need for God and God's way of salvation in Christian teaching, and indeed, in the New Testament itself. In the first view, all human beings are guilty of sinful actions for which they need divine forgiveness. In the second, all humanity is in bondage to "Sin" as a supra-individual, and perhaps supra-human, power from which humanity needs deliverance and liberation. In other words God "saves" human beings by forgiving them, but also, and perhaps even more urgently, God "saves" human beings by delivering them from the forces that divide and destroy humanity, from the compulsion to repeat lethal behaviors on both an individual and corporate scale, and from their inability even to accept forgiveness, let alone their inability to forgive others. As culpable creatures under divine judgment, all people need forgiveness. As creatures enslaved by sin, all people need redemption or liberation. Through both forgiveness and deliverance, God saves humanity from death. All of this is bound up in the notion of "redemption."

These two strands of thought are in some tension with each other; each is well represented in the New Testament, and each has far-reaching implications. Despite the tension, the notions of forgiveness for sin and redemption from sin are mutually informative. Both Luke 15 and Romans 8 demonstrate links between forgiveness and redemption and thus are excellent texts for focusing our discussion of these themes in Christian faith. The Gospel of Luke particularly stresses the theme of forgiveness for sins in its portrayal of Jesus's preaching, and nowhere more richly than in the parable of Luke 15:11–32. And yet Luke also repeatedly emphasizes the good news of Christ's ministry of liberation for the poor, the downtrodden, those at the margins of society, oppressed and enslaved by societal sins. So Luke provides a chance to explore the intersection between forgiveness and redemption, but with an emphasis on forgiveness. In Paul's letters, on the other hand, the dominant theme is not forgiveness for individual sins but liberation from bondage to sin as a hostile power that is opposed to God and opposed to human flourishing. This is perhaps nowhere more strongly stated than in Romans 7–8. And yet earlier in Paul's letter to the churches in Rome, he also talks about divine judgment on human culpability for sin. So in Romans, as in Luke, one finds a link between forgiveness for human wrongdoing and redemption from human bondage to sin. These strands come together in Romans 8:1–4.

## Forgiveness: Luke 15:11–32

Christians traditionally call this the parable of the prodigal son, but close readers note that it really is about the prodigal father. It concerns the character of God as the basis for forgiveness and reconciliation, which are closely related. One of the most familiar of Jesus's parables, the story offers a shocking portrayal of God that can be dimmed by that familiarity. We may sharpen our hearing of this parable by situating it in relationship to other ancient views of parental responsibility toward children. For example, sometime early in the second century BCE, a Jewish sage named Ben Sira gave the following advice:

> To son or wife, to brother or friend,
> do not give power over yourself, as long as you live;
> and do not give your property to another,
> in case you change your mind and must ask for it.
> While you are still alive and have breath in you,
> do not let anyone take your place.
> For it is better that your children should ask from you
> Than that you should look to the hand of your children.
> Excel in all that you do;
> bring no stain upon your honor.
> At the time when you end the days of your life,
> in the hour of your death,
> distribute your inheritance (Sirach 33:20–24).

The logic of Ben Sira is straightforward, and his advice is full of common sense. If parents give their children their inheritance early, then when they are old, they will not have anything to spend on themselves and will have to go begging to their children for their needs. Furthermore, property is tied to status and independence. As Ben Sira says, "Do not let *anyone* have power over you." It is far preferable to be the haves giving to the have-nots, maintaining a position of high status and freedom, than to be in a position of need and therefore of lower status. Furthermore, good parents do not let their children have power over them; they maintain the upper hand, and especially, they keep control of the purse strings. They teach responsible use of money, and they make sure that their children face the consequences of their actions.

Ben Sira demonstrates how countercultural the father's actions are in Jesus's story. This father splits his sons' inheritance while he is still alive, lets his younger son liquidate his share and go out on his own with no good intentions, and then welcomes him back with open arms, no questions asked. This father is a weak and poor parent, according to the received wisdom of his day, and of ours. He is too lax, too generous, too careless of consequences, too trusting. Doing the opposite of what Ben Sira advises, he lets his sons have power over him, he abdicates his own status, and he gives away his property. In a first-century context, the younger son's demand for his inheritance as good as says, "I wish you were dead." Not only does the father acquiesce to this disrespectful demand; when the son comes back as a beggar, the father eases the son's humiliating return by humbling himself instead, throwing aside his dignity and running down the street to greet him. Cutting short his son's confession, demanding no explanations, and imposing no conditions, instead this prodigal father restores the honor of his wayward son by giving him his ring, his robe, and the fatted calf. In Ben Sira's terms, he is weak and shameful as a father.

What are we to make of this tension between Ben Sira and Jesus's parable? I suggest it reveals something about the character of God as a basis for hope in the face of the human propensity to do egregious harm to others and to oneself. The prodigal father operates with a sovereign freedom from preconditions. Out of his mercy and love, he extends forgiveness and reconciliation to the undeserving son, thereby creating the conditions that make full repentance possible. The father's abundance is what prompts the son to repent in the most basic sense of the word, which is to turn back. When the son finally "comes to himself" in the pigsty, he says, "How many of my father's hired hands have enough and to spare?" It is the remembrance that in his father's house there is enough and to spare that brings the son home and opens the door to reconciliation.

There are several aspects of forgiveness here worth pondering. First, forgiveness precedes repentance. Repentance is a response to a gift already given, not a bargaining chip that gains forgiveness. The son does not even have the chance to speak his words of contrition before the father welcomes him back. Something of this is expressed in the words of absolution in the Episcopal Book of Common Prayer:

> The almighty and merciful Lord grant you absolution and forgiveness of all your sins, true repentance, amendment of life, and the grace and consolation of the Holy Spirit.

Here the prayer for "true repentance" follows after the granting of absolution: the fullness of repentance is possible only in the arena of gracious relationship. Furthermore, in the context of grace, the experience of forgiveness and repentance includes a renewed self-knowledge. The younger son "comes to himself" in the pigsty, and there is reason to hope that he further "comes to himself" in his reconciliation with the father. The elder son, on the other hand, has not yet come to himself because he has not experienced forgiveness and repentance. He remains thus far entrapped in bitterness and judgment toward his brother.

Second, forgiveness has an economic aspect to it. In this parable that economy becomes clear in the conversation between the father and the older son. The older son has kept strict account of the losses suffered by his father and himself when his brother took half the family assets. He operates out of a zero-sum economy, with justice on his side. The father, on the other hand, operates out of an economy of abundance. He does not keep tabs. He does not balance the books. He cancels debts. This is just what forgiveness entails, and it is the only way to reconciliation in the story: The son can never repay his debt; cancel it. The old rights of inheritance will impede the inclusion of the alienated son; override them. In this picture the kingdom of God is not about what is earned or deserved but what is freely given to the undeserving.

Third, forgiveness is bound up with reconciliation, which is the restoration of relationship. This is not to say that forgiveness requires such restoration; in the story the father already has forgiven the son, long before the son returns. Forgiveness invites reconciliation; it is not dependent on it. The parable depicts reconciliation received by the younger son and reconciliation refused by the older son, but the attitude of the father is not changed thereby—it remains the same toward both sons.

Fourth, throughout the gospels, forgiveness belongs with God, who alone has authority to forgive sins. Thus, when Jesus forgives sins, it is a cause of amazement and offense, because the forgiveness of sins is a divine prerogative. Two significant examples come to mind here. Earlier in Luke's gospel, Jesus is dining at the home of a Pharisee when a woman with a reputation as a "sinner" enters the house, kneels at Jesus's feet as she anoints them with oil, and wipes them with her hair (Luke 7:36–50). The Pharisee is scandalized. Jesus, however, exalts the woman as an example of forgiveness: "Her sins, which are many, are forgiven, for she loved much; but he who is forgiven little, loves little" (Luke 7:47). Notable here is the connection between forgiveness and relationship, as the acceptance of forgiveness is completed by love. As is common in Luke's gospel, the least deserving, most marginalized character in the story becomes the paragon of faith precisely because she trusts in Jesus as the one who gives to undeserving recipients rather than to the righteous. After this, Jesus tells the woman, "Your sins are forgiven." The other guests respond in shock: "Who is this, who even forgives sins?" His action is an implicit claim to divinity.

In a second example, which occurs in both Mark and Matthew (Mark 2:1–12; Matt. 9:2–8), Jesus is in a house that is so crowded all entrance is blocked. Some men climb up on the roof, remove the tiles, and lower their paralyzed friend down into the crowd in front of Jesus. Jesus says to him, "Your sins are forgiven." Once again, such authority offends the most religious of the bystanders. Then Jesus says, "So that you may know that the Son of Man has authority to forgive sins, I say to you, 'Stand up, take up your pallet, and walk.'" Immediately the man stands up and walks. The point, of course, is that Jesus's divinely given authority extends over both forgiveness and human need. But the story also links forgiveness with healing as deliverance from bondage, including bondage to paralysis.

These stories display the countercultural power of forgiveness, which elevates its lowly recipients and shames those who seem to be above the need for forgiveness (see also the parable of the Pharisee and the tax collector [Luke 18:9–14]). Those who accept forgiveness in turn become capable of extending it to others. Thus there are many instances when Jesus tells people to forgive one another, but that command is always grounded in the forgiveness given by God. In particular, members of the community are to forgive one another "seventy times seven" (Matt. 18:21–22), which may be a command to forgive in countless instances of wrong, or may mean forgiving the same wrong again and again. In either case people are commanded to forgive others who hurt them. What remains unique to God is the authority to forgive all sins because God is the only one with authority to judge and because all sins are ultimately against God.

The climax of Jesus's teaching on forgiveness in Luke comes at the crucifixion, when he says from the cross, "Father, forgive them, for they do not know what they are doing" (Luke 23:34). The authority of this word derives from the one who speaks it, Jesus, who on the cross bears the sins of the world. Thus, if in the parable of Luke 15:11–32 forgiveness is grounded in the character of God as metaphorical father, here on the cross forgiveness is grounded in the life, death, and resurrection of Jesus. That is, forgiveness is bound up not only in Jesus's teachings but also in his actions, in the very shape of his life. It is this very same life, death, and resurrection of Jesus that in turn grounds Paul's teaching on redemption. In Luke's gospel Jesus teaches about forgiveness and accomplishes forgiveness and salvation; in Paul's letters Paul announces the redemption enacted by Jesus.

## Redemption: Romans 8:1–4

The letters of Paul generally are more difficult to read than the gospels. In part this is a matter of genre: gospels are narratives, and the parables present somewhat discrete stories with rich possibilities for interpretation. Paul's letters, on the other hand, occur in the context of his relationships with particular churches, and because they develop complex arguments over the course of the letter, it is difficult to read one short segment out of its larger context. This is certainly the case with Romans 8:1–4, which arguably is the climax of the preceding seven chapters of the letter.

In Romans 1–7 Paul develops a complex and layered account of humanity's need for redemption, including the two views noted earlier: sin as human culpability and sin as enslaving and deceiving power. Sin is a verb—what humans *do*—and sin is a noun that acts as the subject of active verbs—sin does things to and through human beings. In the first section of the letter, Paul preaches that human beings are guilty of the primal idolatry of worshipping the creature rather than the creator and are deserving of judgment and wrath. In this context emphasizing human culpability, deliverance from wrath comes through Christ's expiatory death on behalf of all humanity: "For there is no distinction, since all have sinned and fall short of the glory of God, they are justified by his grace as a gift, through the redemption which is in Christ Jesus, whom God put forward as an expiation by his blood" (Rom. 3:21).

This cultic and judicial language expresses what the Christian reformer John Calvin called the "glorious exchange" and what others have called "interchange in Christ." It has the sense that Christ bore the judgment for sin on behalf of sinful human beings; in so doing, the perfectly righteous Christ exchanged places with sinful humanity. Paul repeats the same idea a bit later in Romans when he says, "God shows his love for us because while we were sinners, Christ died for us. Therefore having been rectified by his blood, how much more shall we be saved by him from the wrath of God" (Rom. 5:8–9). Similarly, in Romans 8:3 Paul proclaims, "God has done what the law, weakened by the flesh, was powerless to do. Sending his own Son in the likeness of the flesh of sin and *for sin*, he condemned sin in the flesh." The phrase "for sin" (*peri hamartias*) occurs in cultic terminology in the Old Testament as the language of a sin offering. The divine judgment on sin has fallen on Jesus Christ so that in him human beings are set free from condemnation for sin (Rom. 8:1). Here Paul comes close to the idea of forgiveness by announcing freedom *from* condemnation and therefore freedom *for* relationship with God and with one another.

The dominant idea in Romans 8, however, is that of redemption, which is not only deliverance from *condemnation for sin* but also freedom from the *compul-*

*sion to sin.* Paul depicts this freedom in terms of relationship; human beings are never on their own, exercising freedom as autonomous individuals, but rather always exist in relationship to others and to God. It is through relationship with God that human beings are set free from sin. This idea of redemption therefore is animated by a logic of divine solidarity with humanity in Christ's incarnation and crucifixion, through which God enters fully into the situation of humanity even to the point of death, thereby bringing all human beings out of death into life. Such a divine rescue mission is necessary because persons of their own power are not capable of breaking the destructive power of sin; it takes God's movement into the human sphere in solidarity with human dereliction to overcome sin and death.

Romans 8:1–4 is one of many places where Paul sets forth this understanding of redemption. Paul's argument is dense and complex, requiring careful disentangling of the role of Christ and the role of the Spirit in setting humanity free. The Son brings liberation from sin through his full solidarity with condemned humanity, even to the point of crucifixion as a condemned criminal; the Spirit brings that liberation to fruitful experience through indwelling the new community that lives "in Christ." Paul unites judicial and redemptive themes here by stressing the participation of the divine Son in human dereliction and culpability under sin, which in turn opens the way for human participation in the life given by God through the Spirit.

A bit later in the chapter, Paul identifies this Spirit as both the Spirit of Christ and the Spirit of God, who raised Jesus Christ from the dead. The Spirit is God's presence within the community of believers, giving them life and peace, uniting them in one family, inspiring prayer and conformation to the image of Christ. All of this is a part of redemption, which includes liberation from sin, transformation into a Christlike life, and the promise of eternal life. At the same time the theme of freedom from condemnation threads through this promise of transformation, as Paul exclaims, "Who shall bring any charge against God's elect? It is God who rectifies: who is to condemn? Is it Christ Jesus, who died, yes, who was raised from the dead, who is at the right hand of God, who indeed intercedes for us?" (8:33b–34).

## Forgiveness and Redemption

There are several common themes uniting Luke's account of forgiveness and Paul's account of redemption. Forgiveness flows from the merciful character of God; it is freely given and creates a gracious relationship that opens the door to repentance as truth telling and reconciliation. Redemption includes forgiveness but extends to a divine act of liberation through God's full participation in the sphere of human dereliction under the sway of sin and death and God's victory over sin and death. Common to both themes is the overarching conviction that salvation is a gift. The Greek word used in the New Testament is *charis*, which is usually translated as "grace." In the ancient Roman systems of patronage and benefaction through which wealthy patrons cemented their social ties, *charis* simply meant "gift"; gifts demonstrated the affluence of the giver and established or strengthened strong social bonds of dependence and obligation. Because of those bonds, givers were careful about choosing recipients: the recipient must be worthy, be fitting, have adequate social status, and not be someone who would be an awkward acquaintance. It is in this respect that the gifted character of forgiveness and redemption is countercultural—certainly in the ancient world, and perhaps today as well. Forgiveness is a gift—but in the gospels, Jesus gives it to the unfitting, the undeserving, the embarrassingly low status. Redemption is a gift, also given precisely to "the ungodly"; as Paul puts it in Romans, the ungodly are "made right with God freely, as a gift." In both cases, the gift instigates a relationship between the recipients and God. We could say that the relationship itself *is* the gift, a gift of unstoppable, gracious presence grounded in the character of the giver.

Finally, in both the gospels and Paul's letters, this divine presence, right in the midst of bodily existence in the realm still dominated by sin and death, is in fact the leverage or power that works redemption. In this way the logic of solidarity is fundamental in Luke as well as Paul. In the gospel, Jesus pronounces forgiveness in his role as God's incarnate presence in space and time. In Paul's letters, that divine participation in the realm of sin and death, and victory over it, generates the interpersonal bond between God and humanity in which human beings are strengthened to overcome sin.

# Divine Forgiveness in Islamic Scripture and Thought

MOHAMMAD HASSAN KHALIL

**WE FIND** in the Qur'ān terrifying descriptions of the fiery torments awaiting sinners and rejecters of faith. The Qur'ān informs us that God is "swift in punishment" (*sarīʿ al-ʿiqāb*) and "severe in punishment" (*shadīd al-ʿiqāb*); "whoever has done an iota of evil will see it" on Judgment Day (al-Zalzala [99]:8). Yet Islamic scripture also draws attention to the forgiving, merciful nature of the Almighty. He is the Loving (*al-Wadūd*), the Forgiving (*al-Ghafūr*), the Peace (*al-Salām*). What is more, at the beginning of nearly every sūra, we read, "*Bismi-l-lāh al-raḥmān al-raḥīm*" (In the name of God, the Lord of Mercy, the Giver of Mercy). The terms *al-raḥmān* and *al-raḥīm* are related to the term *raḥim*, the mother's womb, the center of loving mercy. According to Islamic scripture (for example, in al-Aʿrāf [7]:156), this loving mercy (*raḥma*) encompasses all things; however, it is specially ordained for certain people—the "successful ones" (*al-mufliḥūn*) (al-Aʿrāf [7]:157).

## The Criterion for Success

The Qur'ān presents the criterion for "success" in Sūra 103 (al-ʿAṣr):

> 1By the declining day,
> 2Humanity is [deep] in loss,
> 3Except for those who believe, do good deeds, urge one another to the truth, and urge one another to steadfastness.[1]

The second verse of this brief sūra—the declaration that people are in a state of loss—is unsettling. The following verse, however, offers a critical qualification:

salvation and success awaits those who have faith, "do good deeds, urge one another to the truth, and urge one another to steadfastness." To be sure, even the righteous sin; however, God may choose to pardon them and grant them success on account of their virtuous deeds—deeds that reflect sincerity and true faith.

## Repentance and Forgiveness

Bearing in mind that the Almighty created humans to be fallible, the God of justice and mercy may choose simply to forgive His sinful servants when they repent with sincerity. As we read in Sūrat al-Zumar (39):53–59:

> [53]Say, "[God says], My servants who have harmed yourselves by your own excess, do not despair of God's mercy. God forgives all sins: He is truly the Most Forgiving, the Most Merciful. [54]Turn to your Lord. Submit to Him before the punishment overtakes you and you can no longer be helped. [55]Follow the best teaching sent down to you from your Lord, before the punishment suddenly takes you, unawares, [56]and your soul says, 'Woe is me for having neglected what is due to God, and having been one of those who scoffed!' [57]Or it says, 'If God had guided me, I would have joined the righteous!' [58]Or, faced by punishment, it says, 'If only I could have another chance, I would join those who do good!' [59]No indeed! My messages came to you and you rejected them: you were arrogant and rejected the truth."

Again, that God may choose to pardon the sincere, whatever their sins, is a pronounced theme in the ḥadīth corpus: we find various statements attributed to the Prophet concerning the forgiveness of sinners who mend their ways—or simply intend to mend their ways—before passing away. For instance, in the Ṣaḥīḥ al-Bukhārī ḥadīth collection, we read about a prostitute who used her shoe to collect water for a thirsty dog on the verge of death; on account of this good deed, God forgave her of her sins. We also read about a man who murdered ninety-nine people before seeking to mend his ways. When a monk asserted that he would not be forgiven, the monk became—to put it crudely—victim number one hundred. Eventually, the murderer encountered a man who advised him to seek guidance in a particular village. On the way to the village, the murderer passed away. With the angels disputing whether he should be punished or rewarded, God determined that he would be saved if he had passed away closer to his destination than to his starting point. As it turned out, he had not. Nevertheless, God, out of His mercy, physically moved the destination closer to him so that he would attain salvation.

We also find in the ḥadīth corpus reports of prophets and martyrs interceding on behalf of believers who might have committed numerous transgressions. To reiterate, "God forgives all sins." But as the Qur'ān clarifies in Sūrat al-Nisā', the one sin God does not pardon—at least in the absence of sincere repentance during this life—is *shirk*, or associating partners with God (al-Nisā' [4]:48, 116). This is a cardinal sin because it constitutes an arrogant or negligent rejection of the reality and unity of the Creator, the source of all that is good.

### *Divergent Views on* Shirk*, the Unpardonable Sin*

Many Muslims—theologians included—assume that polytheism and Trinitarianism are *in and of themselves* obvious examples of *shirk*: polytheists associate false deities with God, while Christians associate Jesus with God. This assumption is grounded in a popular reading of the Qur'ān (e.g., al-Mā'ida [5]:72); however, it is not shared by various prominent Muslim theologians.

Consider the case of Abū Ḥāmid al-Ghazālī (d. 1111 CE), arguably the most influential Muslim theologian of all time. In his treatise *Fayṣal al-Tafriqa* (The decisive criterion), al-Ghazālī presents a relatively optimistic vision of life after death. On account of God's overwhelming mercy, al-Ghazālī maintains that only a small minority of humanity—the *truly* wicked—will endure everlasting damnation. Furthermore, considering that God chastises only those who have received and either rejected or ignored the divine message (as can be deduced from passages such as al-Isrā' [17]:15), al-Ghazālī proclaims that God will excuse numerous Christians, namely, those who never heard of the Prophet, those who encountered only false rumors about him, and those who encountered accurate information about him and proceeded to investigate his truth claims before passing away.[2] For al-Ghazālī, their faith in the Trinity would not necessarily qualify as damnable *shirk*. Elsewhere in his writings al-Ghazālī asserts that the Trinity is not in and of itself a violation of monotheism: mainstream Christians, he writes, view the three persons of the Trinity as attributes of the same God.[3] Be that as it may, for al-Ghazālī, belief in the Trinity *could* qualify as true *shirk* if it is accompanied by a conscious rejection of the Qur'ānic message. In this case belief in the Trinity would entail attributing divine qualities to what the Qur'ān teaches is not divine (Jesus) and possibly even divine knowledge to oneself. By the same token anyone who consciously rejects the Qur'ān could also be guilty of *shirk*.[4]

According to al-Ghazālī, true *shirk* entails an attitude of arrogance or negligence toward the divine message following "proper" exposure to it. In the absence of such exposure, non-Muslims are not culpable for their nonbelief. Scholars such as Ibn al-'Arabī (d. 1240 CE) and Muḥammad Rashīd Riḍā (d. 1935) went a step further: both held that God excuses those non-Muslims who, in their heart of hearts, do not find the Islamic message compelling even after having been "properly" exposed to it.[5] And in recent decades Muslim pluralists have averred that God may even save those People of the Book and other non-Muslims who do find the Islamic message compelling yet choose to remain within their respective religious traditions.[6]

## Salvation after Damnation?

As for those individuals whom God does not pardon, they will endure everlasting chastisement—or at least this is the prevailing doctrine in Islamic theology. According to most theologians, sinners with at least an iota of faith in their hearts might have to endure judgment and even punishment in hell for a time, but they will eventually be saved; all others will remain imprisoned in the Fire.

According to some exegetes and theologians, however, even the damned might one day be saved. Consider the wording of Surat al-Anʿām (6):128:

> On the day He [i.e., God] gathers everyone together [saying], "Company of jinn! You have seduced a great many humans," their adherents among humankind will say, "Lord, we have profited from one another, but now we have reached the appointed time You decreed for us." He will say, "Your home is the Fire, and there you shall remain"—unless God wills otherwise (*illā mā shāʾa Allāh*): [Prophet], your Lord is all wise, all knowing.

Notice the exception here: "'Your home is the Fire and there you shall remain'—unless God wills otherwise."

In his final treatise, *Fanāʾ al-Nār* (The annihilation of the Fire), the prominent traditionalist theologian Ibn Taymiyya (d. 1328 CE) points to this passage, among others, as evidence for the ultimate cessation of chastisement. For Ibn Taymiyya the exception, "unless God wills otherwise," qualifies all divine threats of damnation. It also explains why al-Nabāʾ (78):23 states that the transgressors will tarry in hell "for ages" (*aḥqāban*) rather than forever. (Although the Qurʾānic expression *khālidīna fīhā abadan* [al-Jinn (72):23] is typically translated as, "they will remain in it [i.e., Hell] forever," Ibn Taymiyya's student Ibn Qayyim al-Jawziyya [d. 1350 CE] held that a more precise interpretation would be, "they will remain in it for a long time," or "for as long as hell exists.") In contrast the Qurʾān explicitly affirms the continuity of paradise: it is an "unceasing gift" (*ʿaṭāʾan ghayr majdhūdh*) (Hūd [11]:108) whose provisions will "neither be limited nor forbidden" (*lā maqtūʿa wa-lā mamnūʿa*) (al-Wāqiʿa [56]:33).[7]

To be sure, this is a controversial claim and argument. The notion that God might one day save Pharaoh and possibly Satan himself is one that many theologians consider heretical. For them the exception in al-Anʿām (6):128 might simply refer to, among other things, the period preceding damnation, in which case the translation should read, "He will say, 'Your home is the Fire, and there you shall remain'—except whatever [period] God wills." And even if the exception in this verse signifies the temporality of the punishment of the Fire, it does not necessarily signify the temporality of punishment itself: the ḥadīth corpus attests to the existence of other forms of chastisement, such as the biting cold of the *zamharīr* abode.

Although most Muslim scholars held that the Fire must be everlasting, some spoke of salvation *within* it. The Sūfī Ibn al-ʿArabī, for instance, maintained that when the damned eventually submit to God, they will experience "sweetness" (*ʿudhūba*) rather than "punishment" (*ʿadhāb*). They will remain veiled from God, yet they will experience pleasure in, of all places, the flames of hell. In affirming the cessation of chastisement, Ibn al-ʿArabī (in his voluminous *al-Futūḥāt al-makkiyya*) cites Hūd (11):106–8, a passage that is in some ways similar to al-Anʿām (6):128:

> 106The wretched ones will be in the Fire, sighing and groaning, 107There to remain for as long as the heavens and earth endure, unless your Lord wills otherwise (*illā mā shāʾa rabbuka*): your Lord carries out whatever He wills. 108As for those who have been blessed, they will be in Paradise, there to remain as long as the heavens and earth endure, unless your Lord wills otherwise (*illā mā shāʾa rabbuka*)—an unceasing gift.

I should clarify that most exegetes take the expression "for as long as the heavens and earth endure" to mean "forever." Now notice that both the threat of chastisement and the promise of bliss are qualified ("unless your Lord wills otherwise"). But notice also what follows each qualification: while the Qurʾān describes paradise as "an unceasing gift"—an apparent confirmation of everlasting pleasure—it states, "Your Lord carries out whatever He wills" with regard to the damned. According to Ibn al-ʿArabī, although this passage indicates that the damned will remain in the Fire, it never states that the punishment within the Fire will be "unceasing"—an adjective that God reserves for the "gift" awaiting the inhabitants of paradise.[8] Again, with regard to the chastisement, "your Lord carries out whatever He wills."

As I indicated earlier, the prevailing view among Muslim theologians is that at least some people will endure everlasting damnation. To be clear, advocates of this doctrine generally take it as a given that God is overwhelmingly forgiving and merciful. After all, in a well-known ḥadīth, the Prophet declares that God's mercy "overtakes" (and, in a variant report, "outstrips") His wrath.[9] But for these theologians, God—the Just, the Judge, the Omnipotent—turns away from those who turn away from Him; He refuses to forgive those who refuse to seek His forgiveness in this life.

## Forgiveness, Divine and Human

Scriptural accounts of God's willingness to forgive His servants serve various purposes. Needless to say, they provide hope for sinners. They also inspire believers to forgive those who have wronged them. Consider for instance Sūrat al-Nūr (24):22: "Those who have been graced with bounty and plenty should not swear that they will [no longer] give to kinsmen, the poor, those who emigrated in God's way: let them pardon and forgive. Do you not wish that God should forgive you? God is most forgiving and merciful." According to many exegetes, this verse was revealed after the Prophet's companion Abū Bakr swore that he would no longer support a relative of his who had spread rumors about ʿĀʾisha, Abū Bakr's daughter and the Prophet's wife.

This spirit of forgiveness is apparent throughout the ḥadīth corpus, especially in contexts in which the safety of the Prophet's community was not at stake. Consider, for instance, the various reports of the Prophet's treatment of ʿAbd Allāh ibn Ubayy, the leader of the "hypocrites" (*munāfiqūn*) of Medina.[10] According to these reports, ʿAbd Allāh was among the individuals who spread rumors about ʿĀʾisha. He also abandoned the Prophet at ʿUḥud and even plotted to assassinate him. Yet when he passed away, the Prophet eagerly prayed for his forgiveness. As his companion ʿUmar recounted ʿAbd Allāh's transgressions, the Prophet simply smiled. Interestingly, in this case, God, the All-Knowing, informed the Prophet that he had gone too far, not because he had forgiven ʿAbd Allāh himself but because he had prayed to God for ʿAbd Allāh's forgiveness. God informed the Prophet that He would not forgive ʿAbd Allāh on Judgment Day, as he was a man whose unbelief and hypocrisy had become manifest and who passed away without repenting. And yet a lesson that Muslims might deduce from this episode is that, given our limitations of knowledge, it is best to err on the side of forgiveness.

### Notes

1 My translation of the Qurʾān loosely follows that of M. A. S. Abdel Haleem. Here in the second verse I have replaced "Man" with "Humanity." Elsewhere, I replace "mankind" with "humankind."

2 Abū Ḥāmid al-Ghazālī, *On the Boundaries of Theological Tolerance in Islam: Abū Ḥāmid al-Ghazālī's Fayṣal al-Tafriqa*, trans. Sherman A. Jackson (Karachi: Oxford University Press, 2002), 126–28.

3 Ebrahim Moosa, *Ghazālī and the Poetics of Imagination* (Chapel Hill: University of North Carolina Press, 2005), 149.

4 Mohammad Hassan Khalil, *Islam and the Fate of Others: The Salvation Question* (New York: Oxford University Press, 2012), 32.

5 Ibid., chaps. 2 and 4.

6 See Mohammad Hassan Khalil, "Salvation and the 'Other' in Islamic Thought: The Contemporary-Pluralism Debate (in English)," *Religion Compass* 5, no. 9 (2011): 511–19.

7 Khalil, *Islam and the Fate*, chap. 3.

8 William C. Chittick, *Ibn 'Arabi: Heir to the Prophets* (Oxford: Oneworld, 2005), 131–32.

9 This ḥadīth (and its variant) appears in the *Ṣaḥīḥ al-Bukhārī* collection.

10 These reports appear in, among other places, the *Ṣaḥīḥ al-Bukhārī* collection.

# Scripture Dialogues on Forgiveness

**IN THE DIALOGUES** on forgiveness, translations of Bible passages are according to the New Revised Standard Version; translations of Qur'ān passages are by M. A. S. Abdel Haleem.

## DIALOGUE 4

### *Luke 15:11–32*

[11]Then Jesus said, "There was a man who had two sons. [12]The younger of them
said to his father, 'Father, give me the share of the property that will belong to
me.' So he divided his property between them. [13]A few days later the younger son
gathered all he had and travelled to a distant country, and there he squandered his
property in dissolute living. [14]When he had spent everything, a severe famine
took place throughout that country, and he began to be in need. [15]So he went and
hired himself out to one of the citizens of that country, who sent him to his fields
to feed the pigs. [16]He would gladly have filled himself with the pods that the pigs
were eating; and no one gave him anything. [17]But when he came to himself he
said, 'How many of my father's hired hands have bread enough and to spare, but
here I am dying of hunger! [18]I will get up and go to my father, and I will say to
him, "Father, I have sinned against heaven and before you; [19]I am no longer worthy to be called your son; treat me like one of your hired hands."' [20]So he set off
and went to his father. But while he was still far off, his father saw him and was
filled with compassion; he ran and put his arms around him and kissed him.
[21]Then the son said to him, 'Father, I have sinned against heaven and before you;
I am no longer worthy to be called your son.'[22] But the father said to his slaves,
'Quickly, bring out a robe—the best one—and put it on him; put a ring on his

finger and sandals on his feet. [23]And get the fatted calf and kill it, and let us eat and celebrate; [24]for this son of mine was dead and is alive again; he was lost and is found!' And they began to celebrate.

[25]"Now his elder son was in the field; and when he came and approached the house, he heard music and dancing. [26]He called one of the slaves and asked what was going on. [27]He replied, 'Your brother has come, and your father has killed the fatted calf, because he has got him back safe and sound.' [28]Then he became angry and refused to go in. His father came out and began to plead with him. [29]But he answered his father, 'Listen! For all these years I have been working like a slave for you, and I have never disobeyed your command; yet you have never given me even a young goat so that I might celebrate with my friends. [30]But when this son of yours came back, who has devoured your property with prostitutes, you killed the fatted calf for him!' [31]Then the father said to him, 'Son, you are always with me, and all that is mine is yours. [32]But we had to celebrate and rejoice, because this brother of yours was dead and has come to life; he was lost and has been found.'"

## DIALOGUE 5

### *Al-ʿAṣr (103):1–3*

[1]By the declining day, [2]man is [deep] in loss, [3]except for those who believe, do good deeds, urge one another to the truth, and urge one another to steadfastness.

▲ ▲ ▲

### *Al-Zumar (39):53–59*

[53]Say, "[God says], My servants who have harmed yourselves by your own excess, do not despair of God's mercy. God forgives all sins: He is truly the Most Forgiving, the Most Merciful. [54]Turn to your Lord. Submit to Him before the punishment overtakes you and you can no longer be helped. [55]Follow the best teaching sent down to you from your Lord, before the punishment suddenly takes you, unawares, [56]and your soul says, 'Woe is me for having neglected what is due to God, and having been one of those who scoffed!' [57]Or it says, 'If God had guided me, I would have joined the righteous!' [58]Or, faced by punishment, it says, 'If only I could have another chance, I would join those who do good!' [59]No indeed! My messages came to you and you rejected them: you were arrogant and rejected the truth."

▲ ▲ ▲

### *Al-An'ām (6):128*

On the day He gathers everyone together [saying], "Company of jinn! You have seduced a great many humans," their adherents among mankind will say, "Lord, we have profited from one another, but now we have reached the appointed time You decreed for us." He will say, "Your home is the Fire, and there you shall remain"—unless God wills otherwise: [Prophet], your Lord is all wise, all knowing.

## DIALOGUE 6

### *Romans 8:1–4*

There is therefore now no condemnation for those who are in Christ Jesus. [2]For the law of the Spirit of life in Christ Jesus has set you free from the law of sin and of death. [3]For God has done what the law, weakened by the flesh, could not do: by sending his own Son in the likeness of sinful flesh, and to deal with sin, he condemned sin in the flesh, [4]so that the just requirement of the law might be fulfilled in us, who walk not according to the flesh but according to the Spirit.

▲▲▲

### *Hūd (11):106–8*

[106]The wretched ones will be in the Fire, sighing and groaning, [107]there to remain for as long as the heavens and earth endure, unless your Lord wills otherwise: your Lord carries out whatever He wills. [108]As for those who have been blessed, they will be in Paradise, there to remain as long as the heavens and earth endure, unless your Lord wills otherwise—an unceasing gift.

▲▲▲

### *Al-Nabā' (78):21–30*

[21]Hell lies in wait, [22]a home for oppressors [23]to stay in for a long, long time, [24]where they will taste no coolness nor drink [25]except one that is scalding and dark—[26]a fitting requital, [27]for they did not fear a reckoning, [28]and they rejected Our messages as lies. [29]We have recorded everything in a Record. [30]"Taste this: all you will get from Us is more torment."

▲▲▲

### *Al-Aʿrāf (7):40–43*

[40]The gates of Heaven will not be open to those who rejected Our revelations and arrogantly spurned them; even if a thick rope were to pass through the eye of a needle they would not enter the Garden. This is how We punish the guilty—
[41]Hell will be their resting place and their covering, layer upon layer—this is how We punish those who do evil. [42]But those who believe and do good deeds—and We do not burden any soul with more than it can bear—are the people of the Garden and there they will remain. [43]We shall have removed all ill feeling from their hearts; streams will flow at their feet. They will say, "Praise be to God, who guided us to this: had God not guided us, We would never have found the way. The messengers of our Lord brought the Truth." A voice will call out to them, "This is the Garden you have been given as your own on account of your deeds."

## ADDITIONAL QUR'ĀN PASSAGES

During plenary conversation it was the mind of the seminar that Dialogues 5 and 6 would have benefited from the inclusion of the following Qur'ān verses in the booklet of texts to be discussed. They are provided here as translated by the Abdel Haleem translation.

▲▲▲

### *Al-Anʿām (6):12*

Say, "To whom belongs all that is in the heavens and earth?" Say, "To God. He has taken it upon Himself to be merciful. He will certainly gather you on the Day of Resurrection, which is beyond all doubt. Those who deceive themselves will not believe."

▲▲▲

### *Al-Anʿām (6):54*

When those who believe in Our revelations come to you [Prophet], say, "Peace be upon you. Your Lord has taken it on Himself to be merciful: if any of you has foolishly done a bad deed, and afterwards repented and mended his ways, God is most forgiving and most merciful."

▲▲▲

### *Al-Aʿrāf (7):52*

We have brought people a Scripture—We have explained it on the basis of true knowledge—as guidance and mercy for those who believe.

▲ ▲ ▲

### *Al-Muʾminūn (23):109–18*

[109]Among My servants there were those who said, "Lord, We believe. Forgive us
and have mercy on us: You are the most merciful of all." [110]But you kept on laughing at them: so intent were you on laughing at them that it made you forget My
warning. [111]Today I have rewarded them for their patience: it is they who will
succeed. [112]He will say, "How many years were you on earth?" [113]and they will
reply, "We stayed a day or a part of a day, but ask those who keep count." [114]He
will say, "You stayed but a little, if you had only known. [115]Did you think We had
created you in vain, and that you would not be brought back to Us?" [116]Exalted be
God, the true King, there is no god but Him, the Lord of the Glorious Throne!
[117]Whoever prays to another god alongside Him—a god for whose existence he has
no evidence—will face his reckoning with his Lord. Those who reject the truth
will not prosper. [118]Say [Prophet], "Lord, forgive and have mercy: You are the
most merciful of all."

# PART IV

▲ ▲ ▲

# Reconciliation

# Reconciliation Between People

## *Christian Perspectives*

PHILIP SHELDRAKE

**MY OVERALL THEME** in this essay is "reconciliation between people" from a Christian perspective. To nurture a sense of human community and to heal the wounds of division in today's radically plural and often violently divided global culture confront us with the challenge of engaging with inclusivity and diversity, with "otherness" and alienation. These are critical spiritual, as opposed to merely social or political, issues. What does it mean to reconcile otherness? How is human reconciliation to be achieved? A complicated and challenging commitment to reconciliation is vital for human flourishing but is also central to the Christian religious vision. As South African theologian John de Gruchy suggested in his Cambridge University Hulsean Lectures, the doctrine of reconciliation is "the inspiration and focus of all doctrines of the Christian faith."[1]

I want to begin with a few general remarks about what the word *reconciliation* implies and then to make a few introductory comments about some relevant biblical texts. Finally, I will offer some broader reflections on reconciliation from a Christian theological-spiritual perspective.

### The Meaning of *Reconciliation*

First, what does the word *reconciliation* mean? Several concepts are sometimes treated as interchangeable, that is, reconciliation, conciliation, and accommodation or tolerance. Conciliation, or arbitration, is associated with placating our neighbors from whom we are estranged or with negotiations between employers and their workforce. However, conciliation does not necessarily transform people at the deepest level. Accommodation or tolerance is essentially pragmatic: we learn to live alongside the "other" but avoid any significant interchange that may actually change us. This practice has been noted as a weakness in certain versions of multiculturalism in Western countries.[2] In contrast the notion of reconciliation goes much deeper because it suggests harmony, concord, and the healing of deep divisions at a fundamental level. The multivolume edition of the *Oxford English Dictionary* also defines reconciliation historically as "the reconsecration of desecrated places." This refers to buildings, but if we think more provocatively, all those people whose lives are demeaned by what others do or say in contexts of conflict are also "desecrated places" because the sacredness of their identity, as people created in the image of God, is denied.

The theme of reconciliation is a key one in Christianity, but it can sometimes be a somewhat elusive and over-rhetorical notion. In specifically Christian terms, *reconciliation* is not simply a political or psychological word with some incidental theological-spiritual gloss. Protestant Christian approaches emphasize especially reconciliation between God and humanity as a result of Jesus's death on the cross (see Rom. 5:6–11), whereas Catholic Christian approaches often emphasize how the love of God, poured out upon us as a result of divine–human reconciliation, creates a new humanity in which the walls of division between people are broken down (see 2 Cor. 5:17–20, which I will mention later). In fact, both emphases are intimately linked. Interhuman reconciliation is not simply a matter of giving each person his or her rightful due but is ultimately to give God *God's* due, by seeking to build the world that God's all-embracing love demands of us. We should also add a third dimension—that God's act of reconciliation is also intended to overcome the estrangement between humanity and creation.

I will turn my attention briefly to two key texts from the New Testament.

## Gospel of Matthew 18:21–35

This passage from the Gospel of Matthew relates reconciliation specifically to forgiveness. It begins with the apostle Peter's question to Jesus: How often should I forgive someone? Jesus responds with a parable—that is, a brief story that graphically illustrates important religious and ethical teachings. The story recounts how a servant owes his king an incalculable sum of money, cannot pay, begs for more time, and is released from the debt. However, the same servant then refuses to have mercy on a fellow servant who owes him a small amount and imprisons him. In response, the king reimposes the original debt and punishes the first servant. The message is that God's forgiveness is dependent on our willingness to also forgive our fellow humans "from the heart." This echoes a phrase from the Lord's Prayer (the "Our Father")—part of the famous Sermon on the Mount in Matthew, chapter

6: "Forgive us our debts/trespasses as we forgive those who are in debt to us/trespass against us."

A key point is the connection between our treatment of each other and God's treatment of us. Divine forgiveness has been truly appropriated only if it transforms me into a forgiver of others. This was clearly not the case with the servant in the parable. However, this is not proportionate in that God's desire to forgive us far outstrips our limited human conceptions and capacities. Even so, Jesus's initial answer to Peter's "How often should I forgive?" (on one reading, seventy times seven) is that the call to human reconciliation and forgiveness is unquantifiable—beyond immediate calculation. Equally, we must not abuse divine mercy. It may be "infinite" and therefore complete (verse 27), but it is not wholly unconditional. Our forgiveness of others, or commitment to radical reconciliation, is to be "from your heart" (verse 35). We should bear in mind that in late antique Judaism, the image of "the heart" is the true self, the core of our identity.[3] "From your heart" or "wholeheartedly" is therefore not merely something emotional—"with feeling"—but implies reconciliation from our very depths, thus committing the whole self, in contrast to what is superficial, partial, or conditional.

## Letter to the Ephesians 2:11–22

The second New Testament text is part of a letter from the circle associated with the apostle Paul. This letter lays out the radical nature of God's plan for the world as revealed in the life and teachings of Jesus. We are to be a single community. In the first instance being a single community implies the Christian church, which is referred to as the "body of Christ." However, this community does not exist for its own sake or as a citadel protected from the rest of the world. On the contrary, the vocation of the Christian community is to be the prolongation of God's mission to the whole world, and one aspect of this is for the church to be the carrier of, or exemplar of, a new humanity. The *oikumene* of true "ecumenism" means "the whole inhabited world." The world is one in God. Jews and Gentiles, previously separated symbolically by the division of circumcision or noncircumcision (verse 11) and by the observance or nonobservance of religious "law and ordinances" (verse 15), are now made into a single new people—reconciled to each other and to God by God's free action. The universal vocation of the Christian community is perhaps even more clearly laid out in 2 Corinthians 5:18–20. Here the community is given "the ministry of reconciliation"—that is, "we are ambassadors of Christ," proclaiming the message of reconciliation that "in Christ, God was reconciling the world to himself" (verse 19). However, the basis for this mission (verse 20) is that Christians must first accept God's forgiveness themselves and thus be reconciled.

Addressing a Gentile audience, that is, non-Jewish Christians, the Letter to the Ephesians reminds the readers that they were once "aliens from the commonwealth of Israel" and "strangers to the covenants of promise" (verse 12), without hope and without God. However, the very identity of "God's people" is now questioned. The letter assures its audience that they are no longer aliens and strangers in relation to a favored, protected, and exclusive community of insiders but are "citizens with the saints" and "members of the household of God" (verse 19). "All" are "brought near"—a new chosen people (verse 13)—reconciled with God and with the commonwealth of God's people. Mutual hostility is defeated and the dividing wall is broken down (verse 14). The "wall" is undoubtedly one of hostility among human beings but may also refer to a real wall in the Jerusalem Temple that excluded non-Jews from the inner court, thereby preserving religious purity. All people are now given hope and are now connected to God, not through their own merits or capacity but solely by the self-sacrifice ("blood") of Christ. "He [Christ] is our peace" (verse 14).

"He [Christ] has abolished the law with its commandments and ordinances" (verse 15). This does not imply that there is no longer any need for law. However, rather than being merely a series of dry and detached religious regulations and ordinances, "the law" is now embodied in Christ. To observe God's law is to follow the way of Christ and to live out his way of love in our own world.

As a concluding remark, the letters of Paul and his circle present a counterintuitive view of reconciliation. By saying that God is the fundamental agent of reconciliation, the Pauline authors are asserting that *the one who is offended* (by human sin) initiates the process. Normally, in human terms, there is an assumption that a process of reconciliation has to begin with *the offenders* acknowledging their guilt. Here it is God's love, manifested in Jesus Christ, that turns enemies into friends. In the earlier passage from Matthew's gospel, the corollary of this divine dynamic is the challenging call to Christians (and, implicitly, to all humans) to emulate God's character in a love of enemies and the forgiveness of debtors that is not dependent on their rendering prior satisfaction.

## Further Challenging Dimensions

There are a number of other challenging aspects of reconciliation in the Christian scriptures. First, in the letters of Paul and his circle, what lies behind notions of reconciliation, both as God's free and loving action and as a continuing Christian (and more broadly, human) vocation, is what we might call the "parable of beginnings" in the Book of Genesis in the Old Testament, or Hebrew bible. In this story humanity is created by God as God's partner in caring for the world. There is a covenant of trust between God and humanity involving our faithful stewardship of the world in cooperation with God. Also, it is all humanity without exception, created in the image of God, who share a common identity and value as loved and sustained by God. However, human disobedience leads to alienation from God, divisions within the human community (the "walls of separation" in Paul's Letter to the Ephesians), and estrangement from wider nature symbolized in the language of expulsion from the idealized Garden of Eden. This cycle of alienation and estrangement that permeates human existence is encapsulated in a narrative of what is termed "original sin." That is, human nature is inherently flawed and in need of healing. However, out of love, God freely chooses to overcome our sinfulness and to redeem humanity from this cycle of alienation.

Having said this, as humans we exist within a process—a movement *toward* the hope of final restoration and renewal "in God." The notion of a world reconciled by God in Christ does not mean that in our contingent existence evil has already been fully eradicated or that God's kingdom has been finally established. We continue to live out our vocation of reconciliation in a messy and ambiguous world. However, if we follow the message expressed in the letters of Paul and his circle, we are not invited to retreat from the world into some kind of protected, gated, spiritual community—abandoning the wider world to its fate. In that sense, a Christian theology of reconciliation, as originating in God, has profoundly social and ethical implications.

Reconciliation must never become a banal concept. It is not a comfortable word simply promoting an unchallenging, generalized, warm and fuzzy consensus. Interhuman reconciliation, derived from and demanded by God's act of reconciling all things in Christ, is before all else an *action* rather than an abstract doctrine. All discussions about reconciliation must necessarily be concrete and contextual. Reconciliation is always with *these* people, in *this* place, at *this precise moment in time.* Further, it has been noted that Paul's language that we translate as "reconciliation" relates to the Greek verb αλλασσώ, *allasso*—"to exchange." Thus, the concept of reconciliation carries within itself the notion of changing places with the "other," learning to identify with the "other," and being in solidarity with the "other."

## Hospitality

Reflecting on this notion of reconciliation as "changing places," one notices that an important emphasis in both Hebrew and Christian scriptures is on hospitality to the stranger. Many texts in the Hebrew bible make it clear that receiving strangers as if they were our close kin is God's command. An important foundation is for the people of Israel to persistently remember their ancestors' own situation while living as exiles and strangers in Egypt (Deut. 10:19). Part of the narrative of Abraham suggests that his hospitality to three strangers is, unknown to him, actually hospitality to God (Gen. 18). In the New Testament gospels, Jesus himself is frequently portrayed as wandering without a home (e.g., Matt. 8:20) or as depending on the hospitality of others (e.g., Luke 9:58) or as the stranger in our midst (e.g., John 8:14, 25ff.). An important feature of Jesus's own practice was to push his followers away from familiar places into situations they found disturbing. In Mark 6:45, he forces his reluctant disciples into the boat to cross the lake of Galilee to Gentile Bethsaida. In Luke 8:26–39, he healed the demoniac on the east side of the lake in the non-Jewish land of the Gerasenes. In Matthew 15:21–28, Jesus crosses into the land of Tyre and Sidon to heal the daughter of a Canaanite woman and to commend her faith. In Mark 8:1–10, he fed a multitude on the eastern, or non-Jewish, side of the lake. It is worth noting in passing that "otherness" appears in the genealogy of Jesus himself as given in Matthew 1:1–17. This ancestry includes five women, four of whom, apart from his mother Mary, have Gentile connections.

The stranger is not simply someone who is not our kin or is unknown to us. "Strangers" in the Hebrew and Christian scriptures also embrace those who are actively despised or otherwise excluded. In the Gospel of Luke, the obligation in Jewish law both to love God and to love our neighbor "as yourself" as the criteria for inheriting eternal life is presented in a challenging way in the parable of the Good Samaritan. This parable is told in response to a lawyer who challenges Jesus about who is his neighbor (Luke 10:25–37). An anonymous "someone" is attacked by robbers on the road, stripped, and left to die. It is not clear whether this "someone" is a Jewish insider or a stranger. Either way, two religious worthies—a priest and a Levite—pass by, ignore the victim, and do nothing. The person whom Jesus portrays as responding as a true neighbor to the person in need is not one of those bound by the Jewish law but a member of a despised and outcast religious group known as Samaritans.

Thus, Jesus's teaching on hospitality is regularly sharp and challenging. Hospitality is to dignify someone with respectful recognition. Thus, in Luke 14:12–14, Jesus suggests to his host at a dinner that he should not just invite those who might reciprocate and are able to do so but that his invitations to dine should embrace the poor, the crippled, the lame, and the blind who cannot repay him.

Hospitality to the stranger is also presented as having a bearing on our eternal destiny in the portrayal of the final judgment in Matthew 25:31–46. The criterion of judgment is whether we have granted recognition and hospitality to "the least"—the hungry, the stranger, the naked, the sick, or the imprisoned. Jesus's challenging teaching is that these "least" are members of God's family (verse 40); in welcoming or assisting them, we welcome God, and in failing to respond to them, we also reject God (verse 45).

## Hospitality and Reconciliation: Rule of Saint Benedict and Eucharist

In the final part of this essay, I want briefly to develop the image of hospitality to the stranger in relation to two other Christian resources for what might be called a spirituality of reconciliation. The first is the sixth-century monastic Rule of Saint Benedict, and the second is the central Christian ritual of the Eucharist.

The Rule of Saint Benedict, one of the most influential texts in Western Christian spirituality, has a great deal to offer in terms of a Christian approach to promoting reconciliation.[4] The Rule has a number of elements, but here I will focus on only one—the virtue of hospitality. Chapter 53 of the Rule states that all guests who arrive are to be received "as Christ"—in the original Latin, "*Omnes supervenientes hospites tamquam Christus suscipiantur*." The Rule goes on to say, "For he himself will say, I was the stranger and you took me in." Christ is *in* the stranger. Commentators on the Rule have always noted the word *omnes*, "all." This portrays an inclusivity linked particularly to *strangeness*, or we might say "otherness," in contrast to those who are "one of us." *Supervenientes*, "those who arrive," underlines the point even more strongly. It literally means those who "turn up unexpectedly." However, this is not a question merely of those who did not warn us that they were coming to visit but of those who are a surprise to us in a deeper and more disturbing sense. Close to the surface of the text is the understanding that Christians are not to be choosey about whom they keep company with. The word *hospites* is ambiguous and can legitimately be translated as "strangers" as well as "guests." The former sense is reinforced by the reference in the Rule to the last judgment narrative of Matthew 25:35: "I was a stranger and you took me in." Finally, the word *suscipiantur* literally means "to be received," but its deeper sense is "to be cherished" or loved. Thus, the stranger is someone who, while different from us, we must learn to value as closely as if he or she were one of our own kin. In the Rule of Saint Benedict, hospitality is a blending of inside and outside worlds. It creates a liminal space in which those who are "other" are genuinely encountered and in which socially ingrained differences are transcended.

Christians enact their theology and spirituality of reconciliation in the central ritual meal of sharing the Eucharist. Unfortunately, some approaches to a theology and practice of the Eucharist are too comfortable. They concentrate on building up the Christian community in and for itself. As Bolivian theologian Victor Codina comments, it is possible to limit reconciliation to a magic circle of people whose worlds overlap to a reasonable degree.[5] However, this bypasses the *risk* inherent in celebrating the Eucharist. The ritual of blessing bread and wine and sharing them is an active memorial of what is known as the Last Supper—that is, the meal that the gospels say that Jesus shared with his disciples before his arrest and death. In Christian belief this memorial action makes present in and for the community of every age the transformative and challenging power of God manifested in Jesus's life, suffering and death, resurrection, and union with God.

The Eucharist is not simply a Christian practice of religious piety but the enactment of the particular identity of the Christian community for the sake of wider humanity. As such, a link between the Eucharist and ethical behavior is intrinsic.[6] The Eucharist powerfully engages the worshipping community with the power of God's forgiveness but through this also with the call to a radical change in our relationships with others. This necessarily challenges the community to undertake appropriate ways of living in the world and promotes a reordering of the existential situations in which we live. We are challenged to set aside our flawed, not least self-contained, identities in favor of something that is offered to us by God's grace, for in the words of Archbishop Rowan Williams, "where we habitually are is not, after all, a neutral place but a place of loss and need" that needs to be transformed.[7] The transforming dynamic of the Eucharist demands that the presumed identity of everyone is to be radically reconstructed. This necessitates an honest recognition of what is wrong with the human condition as well as a process of painful dispossession and fearless surrender as a precondition of reconciliation.

One of the most powerful human symbols of radical hospitality and of reconciliation is to "share the table." During his lifetime Jesus was criticized for having meals with outsiders—eating with publicans (i.e., tax collectors for the Roman authorities) and sinners (see Luke 5:30). Even more powerfully, we know from the gospel narratives that at the Last Supper Jesus shared his final meal not only with disciples like Peter, who would later deny and desert him, but with Judas, who went on to actively betray him. The ritual of the Eucharist is a landscape of memory—including ambiguous or conflicting memories. The central narrative, that is, the revelation of God's redemption of the human condition in the suffering and death of Jesus Christ, embraces all human stories and yet at the same time reconfigures them. The narrative of God's action, ritualized in the Eucharist, makes space for a new narrative that pushes us beyond the exclusions of our various human divisions and separations. This invites us to undertake the radical business of reconciliation and of creating an inclusive human solidarity.

The narrative of God's redemptive work, actively recalled at every Eucharist, tells a very different story from the one shaped by human divisions. There is, therefore, a perpetual and uncomfortable tension in this regular Christian ritual practice between God's reconciling power, on the one hand, and the many efforts of Christians, on the other hand, to resist the call to human reconciliation. The call to Christians at every Eucharist, echoing the text from the Letter to the Ephesians cited earlier, is to "share the table" with, and to be in solidarity with, people they have not chosen, whose presence they have not negotiated, would not choose of their own free will, and may even find distasteful.[8]

A Christian spirituality shaped by the practice of the Eucharist involves a belief that our true identities are determined by God and God's affirming and life-giving gaze rather than by our limited presuppositions and capacities to accept the identity of the "other." The demands on Christians who practice the ritual of the Eucharist are consequently more powerful than any notion of human solidarity based solely on a social or political theory, however inclusive or just this seeks to be.[9]

## Conclusion

By way of conclusion, the vocation of proclaiming human reconciliation is not incidental to Christian life but lies at its very heart. Being in relationship with anyone at all is a risky commitment to others enabled solely by the power of God's unconditional love for humankind. This commitment is expressed by our struggles to stay together in our differences, even in our disputes, within a single human "common home" that is of God's making.

## Notes

1 John de Gruchy, *Reconciliation: Restoring Justice* (London: SCM Pres), 44.

2 See the critical comments of the former British chief rabbi, Dr. Jonathan Sachs, in his *The Home We Build Together: Recreating Society* (London: Continuum, 2007), chaps. 17 and 20.

3 See Peter Brown, "Late Antiquity," in *A History of Private Life*, ed. Paul Vayne, vol. 1, *From Pagan Rome to Byzantium* (Cambridge, MA: Harvard University Press, 1996).

4 There are several good editions of the Rule of Saint Benedict with translations and scholarly commentaries. One of the best is Terrence C. Kardong OSB, ed., *Benedict's Rule: A Translation and Commentary* (Collegeville, MN: Liturgical Press, 1996).

5 Victor Codina, "Sacraments," in *Systematic Theology: Perspectives from Liberation Theology*, ed. Jon Sobrino and Ignacio Ellacuria (London: SCM Press, 1996), 218–19.

6 On this point, see Donald E. Saliers, "Liturgy and Ethics: Some New Beginnings," in *Introduction to Christian Ethics: A Reader*, ed. Ronald Hamel and Kenneth Himes (New York: Paulist Press, 1989), 175–86.

7 Rowan Williams, *On Christian Theology* (Oxford: Blackwell, 2000), 209–10.

8 See Williams, "Sacraments of the New Society," in ibid.

9 Ibid., 212–14.

# Reconciliation and Peacemaking in the Qur'ān

ASMA AFSARUDDIN

**ONE OF THE BEST-KNOWN** verses in the Qur'ān with significant implications for individual transformation and growth and, ultimately, social reform states, "Indeed, God does not change people's circumstances unless they change what is in themselves" (al-Ra'd [13]:11).[1] According to this verse, change is to be effected internally in the individual before any meaningful external change can take root. From the Qur'ānic perspective, the most important site for bringing about genuine individual change followed by social change is thus clearly the human heart—to be understood, of course, not merely as a physical organ but as the basic cognitive and emotive center of the human system.

An important consequence of the human heart's transformation to make it receptive to God's will is the cultivation of fraternal bonds among fellow believers and the effecting of genuine reconciliation between erstwhile enemies. The centrality of harmonious relationships and the importance of maintaining concord among believers is asserted in al-Ḥujurāt (49):10: "The believers are brothers, so make peace between your two brothers and be mindful of God, so that you may be given mercy." The next two verses stress that believers should be mutually respectful and courteous in their speech and not engage in critical and malicious gossip about one other. Such socially destructive behavior stirs up resentment and ill will and undermines the bonds of fraternity and cordiality that must characterize relations among believers.

An incipient methodology of effecting reconciliation and fostering peaceful relations among people may be deduced from two other significant Qur'ānic verses: Āl 'Imrān (3):103 and al-Anfāl (8):63. These two verses refer to "the joining/bringing together [and therefore reconciliation] of hearts," a process that became known in the extra-Qur'ānic literature as *ta'līf al-qulūb* in Arabic. Through the centuries Muslim scholars and theologians have taken note of these crucial verses and focused on their conciliatory implications in their particular sociohistorical contexts as well as in their general applicability, as our following discussion reveals. Other verses—al-Anfāl (8):61, al-Mumtaḥina (60):7–9, al-Ḥujurāt (49):13—that have a considerable bearing on the topic of reconciliation are also discussed in this context.

## Exegeses of Āl ʿImrān 3:103

> Hold fast, one and all, to the "rope of God" and let nothing divide you. Remember the grace of God towards you: when you were enemies He joined your hearts and you became through His grace brothers. (Āl ʿImrān [3]:103)

The famous medieval exegete Muḥammad b. Jarīr al-Ṭabarī (d. 923) understands the phrase "the rope of God" in this verse to be the equivalent of "the religion of God which He has commanded you to follow," and as a consequence of obedience to this command, believers are vouchsafed "cordiality [among them], unity based upon the word of Truth, and submission to God's commandment."[2] He understands the exhortation "Remember the grace of God" to mean "remember the blessing that He conferred on you of friendship and of being gathered together in Islam." He comments further, "Remember! O believers, the bounty of God towards you when you were enemies while polytheists. You killed one another out of tribal partisanship in disobedience to God and His messenger. Then God joined your hearts in Islam (submission [to God]) and made you the brothers of one another after you were enemies and you continue in the bonds of friendship in submission to God."[3]

Al-Ṭabarī provides the occasion of revelation that links the meaning of this verse to the specific situation of two key Medinan tribes before and after the advent of Islam. The enmity referred to in this verse is the enmity that existed in the pre-Islamic period between these two tribes, known as al-Aws and al-Khazraj, as a result of the continuous wars between them. As the pre-Islamic Ayyām al-ʿArab (the battle days of the Arabs) literature informs us, these wars lasted for about 120 years. Al-Ṭabarī refers to Ibn Isḥāq (d. 767), the famous biographer of the Prophet Muḥammad, who recalled that these wars took place between al-Aws and al-Khazraj even though they were closely related. According to Ibn Isḥāq, the intensity of their enmity was unprecedented; however, as al-Ṭabarī quotes him, "Then God Almighty extinguished that [their enmity] through Islam and brought them together through His messenger, Muḥammad, peace and blessings be upon him."[4] Through this verse, al-Ṭabarī affirms, God was reminding the Anṣārī (the Helpers, a reference to the Medinan Muslims) of the misery and wretchedness that had afflicted them on account of their mutual hostility and fear and had led to the shedding of each other's blood. The verse is a further reminder of how submission to God and the guidance of the Prophet finally led to reconciliation and security and facilitated the development of the bonds of friendship and brotherhood between them.[5]

Al-Ṭabarī concludes this section by commenting on the last part of Āl ʿImrān (3):103: "and you became brothers by His grace." This means, he remarks, "Because God, exalted is He, joined your hearts by means of Islam and the word of Truth. Through cooperation in aiding the people of faith and rallying against unbelievers who opposed you—so that there remained no malice and no enmity between you—you became sincere, truthful brothers."[6]

The thirteenth-century Andalusian exegete al-Qurṭubī (d. 1273) understands the "rope of God" mentioned at the beginning of Āl ʿImrān (3):103 to refer to the Qur'ān as well as to communal life. Al-Qurṭubī remarks that the meanings are intertwined and related, for God has enjoined sociability and forbidden separation from the community: "separation is [equivalent to] destruction and communal affiliation is [equivalent to] salvation."[7]

The prohibition "do not become disunited" warns against the divisiveness that can afflict religious communities in the practice of their religion and exhorts believers to remain brothers in "the religion of God" by not blindly following every whim and fancy. Al-Qurṭubī goes on to clarify, however, that the verse does not rule out differences with regard to secondary matters of religion (*al-furūʿ*). If such differences do not lead to dissension and arise in the course of extrapolating legal rulings from and explicating the religious law, then they are not harmful in themselves. The Companions of the Prophet often differed with one another on the derivation of legal rulings in new circumstances, but in spite of that, they remained amicable toward one another. Al-Qurṭubī cites the well-known ḥadīth "The difference of my community is a mercy." The kind of difference God forbids is the kind that leads to corruption and sectarianism.[8]

In his commentary on Āl ʿImrān (3):103, the popular fourteenth-century exegete Ibn Kathīr (d. 1352) similarly stresses the "joining of hearts" that can come about even among the bitterest of enemies when humans are open to the transformative power of God's love in our relations with one another. He points to the Aws and Khazraj tribes that were prone to much fighting in the Jāhiliyya (the pre-Islamic period) and that harbored virulent hatred toward one another. All that was to change, however, "when God brought forth Islam, and those who entered it, entered it and became brothers, loving one another through the majesty of God, cooperating with one another in a spirit of piety and God-consciousness."[9] Ibn Kathīr further points to the danger inherent in relaxing one's guard against potential fractiousness and thus allowing seditious elements to stir up enmity. He relates an anecdote in exegesis of Āl ʿImrān (3):103, according to which an individual of ill will, who was displeased to see the concord and amity reigning among the Aws and Khazraj tribes in Medina, dispatched one of his cohorts to sit among them and revive the memory of their prolonged wars during the Jāhiliyya. The man did as he was told, and before long he had succeeded in inflaming the passions of the Aws and Khazraj to the extent that they started chanting their battle slogans from the pre-Islamic period and reaching for their weapons. News of this reached the Prophet, and he hurriedly approached them and began to calm them down. He asked, "Are you harking back to the pre-Islamic period while I am among you?" Then he recited to them Āl ʿImrān (3):103, at which they were filled with remorse. They began to make up with one another and embraced one another after having cast away their weapons.[10]

This report cogently demonstrates the recuperative power of the remembrance of God and His limitless grace toward humans, which effaces the memory of past wrongs and allows for forgiveness and reconciliation to occur among the bitterest of enemies. But, it also warns, such memories can be resurrected by those malignantly inclined to sow dissension. The constant invocation of God in gratitude for His immeasurable benevolence toward humankind is, however, a potent shield against the incitements of troublemakers and helps preserve the unity of the believers.

The nineteenth-century Muslim reformer and scholar Muḥammad ʿAbduh (d. 1905) similarly stresses in the context of this verse the reconciliation of the Aws and Khazraj tribes of Medina after their submission to God, putting an end to their bitter past of chronic hostility. He further understands this verse to contain a strong denunciation of the tribal partisanship of the pre-Islamic period, termed in Arabic *al-ʿaṣabiyya*. He marshals as proof text the ḥadīth in which the Prophet declares, "One who invokes tribal partisanship is not one of us."[11] ʿAbduh sees this pre-Islamic tribalism resurgent in the nationalisms of his own time that create dangerous divisions among people. He asserts that the true advancement of a nation lies in uniting all its citizens through their devotion to God, which ensures the well-being and welfare of all people, regardless of their religion or ethnicity.[12] It is through "holding fast to God's rope" that one may successfully resist the divisiveness and sectarianism that leads to the shedding of blood, as happened in the pre-Islamic past, and thereby achieve genuine reconciliation among people.

## Exegeses of al-Anfāl (8):63

> And He has joined [or reconciled] their hearts. If you had spent all that is in the earth, you could not have joined their hearts, but God has united them. Indeed He is Almighty, All-Wise. (al-Anfāl [8]:63)

The exegeses of this verse are very similar to those for Āl 'Imrān (3):103. Most commentators, like al-Ṭabarī, al-Qurṭubī, and Ibn Kathīr, understand this verse to be a reference to the Aws and Khazraj tribes and the healing of their bitter past and mutual forgiveness after they had become believers as well as to the brotherly love that was created between the Meccan Emigrants and the Medinan Helpers in the post-Hijra period. The verse is furthermore understood to stress that only God when He enters our hearts can effect this kind of transformation. Thus, al-Ṭabarī comments that this verse addresses the Prophet and reminds him, "Were you to spend, O Muhammad, all that is on earth of gold, money, and worldly goods, you would not be able to reconcile their hearts with all your strength, for it is God Who joins them in guidance!"[13]

Al-Ṭabarī refers to the earlier Medinan exegete Mujāhid b. Jabr (d. 720), who extrapolated a general mandate for reconciliation and peacemaking from this verse. Thus, Mujāhid says that the statement "Were you to spend all that is on earth you would not be able to reconcile their hearts" means that when two Muslims meet and shake hands, their sins are forgiven. A variant exegesis attributed to Mujāhid offers further clarification of this somewhat elliptical comment. According to this variant, a man named 'Abda b. Abī Lubāba related that he met Mujāhid and the latter took his hand in his own and said, "If you should see two individuals who harbor love for God and one of them takes the hand of the other and smiles at him, their sins drop off them just as the leaves drop from the tree." 'Abda told Mujāhid, "But indeed that is easy." Mujāhid remarked, "Do not say that, for indeed God has stated, 'Were you to spend all that is on earth you would not be able to reconcile their hearts.'"[14]

The two reports taken together convey Mujāhid's conviction that sincere faith in God results in genuine bonds of friendship and goodwill among believers, expressed outwardly in gestures of friendship toward one another, such as shaking hands and exchanging smiles. But simply going through such motions does not automatically create a sense of bonhomie unless the believers are firmly embedded in faith and love for God—this latter being a much harder task, as pointed out by Mujāhid. Faith and love for God can only be effected by God Himself. Once firmly implanted in one's heart, love for God translates into love for one's fellow beings.

Muḥammad ʿAbduh understands this verse to apply primarily to the Meccan Muslims, who became brothers of the Medinan Muslims in faith, despite differences in social status and worldly rank. He underscores this dramatic transformation in the following way: "As for the Muhājirun, reconciliation [*taʾlif*] occurred among their rich and the poor, their masters and their clients, their nobility and their common people, in spite of the arrogance of the Jāhiliyya that had previously existed among them."[15] It was this concord among them that allowed them to endure the enmity of their fellow tribesmen and relatives for the sake of God. None of this could have been achieved by means of all the wealth and enticements of the world.

ʿAbduh then goes on to point to the centrality of love in human relationships, which has been, he says, asserted by wise people through the ages. These sages agree that "love is the greatest of all bonds among humans and the most potent inducement to happiness is human social life and its refinement."[16] They further concur that in the absence of love, nothing else can take its place in repelling evil, while the proper functioning of society is contingent on the dispensation of justice. While love has been considered instinctual and not a matter of choice and justice has been regarded as an act of deliberation, Islam made love a virtue and adherence to justice an obligatory duty. Justice in particular was the due of all who reside in the Islamic state, with no distinction made between the Muslim and non-Muslim, pious and impious, rich and poor, and so forth.[17]

In this important exegesis, ʿAbduh goes further than his premodern predecessors and extends the concept of reconciliation based on love and justice to all human beings, regardless of their religious affiliation (or lack thereof). He argues that out of love for the Creator and adherence to justice, the individual and the state must treat everyone evenhandedly.[18]

## Al-Anfāl (8):61

The quintessential Qurʾānic verse concerning peacemaking is Sūrat al-Anfāl (8):61, which exhorts Muslims to make peace with those who are equally inclined to peace. It states,

> If they incline toward peace, incline you toward it, and trust in God. Indeed, He alone is all-hearing, all-knowing.

Al-Ṭabarī says that God in this verse addresses the Prophet and counsels him that if he should fear treachery and perfidy on the part of a group of (unspecified) people (*qawm*), then he should withdraw from them and fight them. But "if they should incline to making peace with you and abandon warfare, either through entry into Islam, or payment of the *jizya*, or through the establishment of friendly relations, then you should do the same for the sake of peace and peacemaking."[19] Al-Ṭabarī considers the commandment to incline to peace to be valid for all times and places. The rest of the verse, concludes al-Ṭabarī, assures the Prophet that he need only place his faith in God when making peace with hostile groups, for He hears and knows all.[20]

The celebrated late-twelfth-century exegete Fakhr al-Dīn al-Rāzī (d. 1210) briefly comments that after the preceding verse (al-Anfāl [8]:60) had exhorted Muslims to assemble their forces against the enemy, Muslims were commanded to accept an offer of peace from the same enemy, should he incline to peace. This commandment remains in effect and has a broad and general applicability.[21]

Al-Qurṭubī similarly remarks that if the adversary inclines to peaceful relations and agrees to peacemaking (*al-ṣulḥ*), then Muslims should also incline to it. The word *al-salm*, as occurs in this verse, and the related word *al-salām* are the equivalents of *al-ṣulḥ* and therefore have to do with peace and peacemaking in general.[22] Al-Qurṭubī refers to unnamed sources who in their exegeses of this verse pointed to the example of the Companions of the Prophet during the time of ʿUmar b. al-Khaṭṭāb and rulers after him who made peace with numerous non-Arab nations through formal treaties, following the precedent of the Prophet Muḥammad.[23] According to a ḥadīth recorded by al-Bukhārī, Muslims may make peace with non-Muslims of all stripes and conclude truces with them without levying any taxes on them. Furthermore, they may conclude peace agreements according to which they themselves pay tribute to the enemy, all in the interest of forging peaceful relations with former adversaries.[24]

## Al-Mumtaḥina (60):7–9

Sūrat al-Mumtaḥina (60):7–9 states,

> Perhaps God will place affection between you and those who are your enemies for God is powerful and God is forgiving and merciful. God does not forbid you from being kind and equitable to those who have neither made war on you on account of your religion nor driven you from your homes; indeed God loves those who are equitable. God forbids you, however, from making common cause with those who fight you on account of your religion and evict you from your homes and who support [others] in driving you out. Those who make common cause with them are wrongdoers.

Al-Ṭabarī says that al-Mumtaḥina (60):7 refers to those among the pagan Meccans who embraced Islam and consequently became the friends and allies of Muslims. The verse goes on to declare that God is certainly capable of planting such affection among people, and He is forgiving and merciful toward those polytheists who repent of their sins. God further commands Muslims to treat with kindness and justice those among the Meccans who do not fight them nor expel them from their homes. According to the most common occasion of revelation given for this verse, it is a reference to Asmāʾ bint Abī Bakr (daughter of the first caliph, Abū Bakr, and sister of ʿĀʾisha, wife of the Prophet), whose mother, Qutayla bint ʿAbd al-ʿUzzā, had not converted to Islam. When Qutayla once came bearing gifts for Asmāʾ, the latter spurned them and prevented the former from entering into her presence, "unless the Messenger of God, peace and blessings be upon him, were to give permission." ʿĀʾisha mentioned the event to the Prophet, and subsequently, al-Mumtaḥina (60):8 was revealed enjoining kindness to peaceful non-Muslims.[25]

Al-Ṭabarī weighs in at this point and stresses that the most appropriate exegesis of this verse is as follows: God has not forbidden Muslims from acting kindly and fairly with all those from any and every religion and creed who do not fight them and do not expel them from their homes. He also summarily dismisses the opinion of some exegetes that this verse is abrogated. The verse should be understood instead as clearly permitting the faithful to always be kind to non-Muslims, whether blood relatives or not, who bear no ill will toward Muslims and as long as such relationships do not compromise the security of Muslims. The truth of his commentary, says al-Ṭabarī, is borne out by the cause of revelation concerning Asmāʾ bint Abī Bakr and her mother. For God loves those who are equitable (*al-munṣifīn*) in their dealings with people, give people their due rights, are personally just to them, and do good to those who are good to them.[26] As for al-Mumtaḥina (60):9, it forbids believers from helping and befriending those from among the unbelievers in Mecca who fight them over religion and evict them from their homes and who clearly represent a source of danger and unmitigated harm to believers. Those among the Muslims who form alliances with such overtly hostile groups are wrongdoers and violate the command of God.[27]

The well-known twelfth-century exegete al-Zamakhsharī (d. 1144) comments that al-Mumtaḥina (60):7 showed concern for those Muslims who had severed their relations with their pagan relatives. They were consequently offered the hope of reconciliation and renewal of affection between them by the revelation of this verse.[28] The next two verses counsel goodness toward those Meccan pagans who did not evince hostility toward Muslims and requires Muslims to continue to give charity to their peaceful pagan relatives, stresses al-Zamakhsharī. He concludes by emphasizing that the command *wa-tuqsiṭū* (Be just!) in al-Mumtaḥina (60):8

requires Muslims to treat non-Muslims justly and refrain from oppression, which he describes as "an excellent command."[29]

Al-Rāzī's exegetical remarks are very similar; he comments that these verses make evident that Muslims are enjoined to show kindness and charity toward non-Muslims who are not belligerent toward them. They furthermore require Muslims to behave justly with non-Muslims, whether they are kinsfolk or not, and to honor their agreements with them.[30] Among the post-Ṭabarī exegetes surveyed, al-Qurṭubī is the most explicit and adamant in maintaining that the exhortation in al-Mumtaḥina (60):8 to be kind to those who had caused Muslims no harm was applicable to everyone who belonged in this category, regardless of their religious affiliation, and that the command was unambiguous and valid for all times.[31]

Moving beyond the Abrahamic communities, a more general injunction to engage with all peoples everywhere, irrespective of faith, ethnicity, culture, and so forth, so as to engender mutual knowledge and understanding may be extrapolated from al-Ḥujurāt (49):13, which states,

> O mankind! We have created you from a male and a female, and made you into nations and tribes, that you might get to know one another. The noblest of you in God's sight is the one who is most righteous.

At the basic semantic level, this verse can be understood to advocate that humans should proactively get to know one another (*li-taʿārafū*), irrespective of their backgrounds, and to remind us that individuals find esteem before God only on the basis of piety. In our own times this verse is understood to be highly significant within a holistic discussion of Qurʾānic perspectives on dialogic encounters. Because of the more parochial circumstances of their own time, medieval exegetes tended to gloss the Arabic verb *taʿārafū* contained in this verse to mean learning about each other's tribal and similar affiliational backgrounds in order to establish bonds of kinship and affection. In explanation of *taʿārafū*, al-Ṭabarī, for example, glosses it as commanding people to get to know one another so that they may discover their bonds of kinship. He warns that knowledge of such kinship is not meant to induce any sense of superiority but rather "to bring you closer to God, for indeed only the most pious among you is the most honorable."[32] Ibn Kathīr, in his exegesis of this term, cites a ḥadīth in which the Prophet states, "Learn about each other's pedigrees so as to establish your blood-ties, for it is such ties which lead to love among people."[33]

Today we can expand the exegetical purview of the verb *taʿārafū* in this verse to extend to not just our blood relatives but all the coresidents of the global village we are now beginning to regard as our shared home, thus realizing more fully the pluralist potential of this verse. In our contemporary circumstances, al-Ḥujurāt

(49):13 may be understood as representing the overall objective of our interfaith and intercultural conversations—to broaden the common ground we inhabit as human beings and to learn about one another as inhabitants of different countries, cultures, and faith communities, with an appreciation for these differences that enrich our lives. Such a dialogic process also leads to self-disclosure and self-understanding, a necessary correlate of the process of mutual illumination, transformation, and, ultimately, genuine reconciliation.

## Notes

1 All translations of Qurʾānic verses are mine.

2 Al-Ṭabarī, *Jāmiʿ al-bayān fī tafsīr al-Qurʾān* (Beirut: Dār al-kutub al-ʿilmiyya, 1997), 3:378.

3 Ibid.

4 Ibid., 7:78.

5 Ibid.

6 Ibid., 7:84.

7 Al-Qurṭubī, *Al-Jāmiʿ li-aḥkām al-Qurʾān* (Cairo: Dār wa-maṭābiʿ al-shaʿb, n.d.), 2:1401.

8 Ibid., 2:1402 ff.

9 Ibn Kathīr, *Tafsīr al-Qurʾān al-ʿazīm* (Beirut: Dar al-jīl, 1990), 1:368.

10 Ibid.

11 Muḥammad ʿAbduh, *Tafsīr al-manār* (Cairo: Maṭbaʿat al-manār, 1931), 4:21.

12 Ibid.

13 Al-Ṭabarī, *Jāmiʿ al-bayān*, 6:280.

14 Ibid., 6:280–81.

15 ʿAbduh, *Tafsīr al-manār*, 10:70–71.

16 Ibid., 71.

17 Ibid.

18 For a fuller discussion of the concept of "reconciliation of hearts," see my chapter "Taking Faith to Heart: Reconciliation and Peacebuilding in Islam," in *Spiritual Dimensions of Bediuzzaman Said Nursi's Risale-I Nur*, ed. Ibrahim Abu Rabiʿ (Albany: State University of New York Press, 2008), 213–29.

19 Al-Ṭabarī, *Jāmiʿ al-bayān*, 6:278.

20 Ibid., 6:278–79.

21 Al-Rāzī, *al-Tafsīr al-kabīr* (Beirut: Dar iḥyāʾ al-turāth al-ʿarabī, 1999), 5:500–501.

22 Al-Qurṭubī, *Jāmiʿ*, 8:40–41.

23 Ibid., 8:42.

24 Ibid.

25 See, for example, Ibn Saʿd, *al-Ṭabaqāt al-Kubrā* (Beirut: Dār ṣādir, 1998), 8:252.

26 Ibid., 12:63.

27 Ibid.

28 Al-Zamakhsharī, *al-Kashshāf ʿan ḥaqā'īq ghawamiḍ al-tanzīl wa-ʿuyūn al-aqāwīl fī wujūh al-taʾwīl*, ed. ʿĀdil Aḥmad ʿAbd al-Mawjūd and ʿAlī Muḥammad Muʿawwaḍ (Riyadh: Maktabat al-ʿubaykn, 1998), 6:92–93.

29 Ibid., 6:94–95.

30 Ibid.

31 Al-Qurṭubī, *Jāmiʿ*, 18:54.

32 Al-Ṭabarī, *Jāmiʿ al-bayān*, 11:398.

33 Ibn Kathīr, *Tafsīr*, 4:218

# Scripture Dialogues on Reconciliation

**IN DIALOGUES** 7, 8, and 9, translations of Bible passages are according to the New Revised Standard Version. The M. A. S. Abdel Haleem translation is provided for Qur'ān passages.

## DIALOGUE 7

### *Matthew 18:21–35*

[21]Then Peter came and said to him, "Lord, if another member of the church sins against me, how often should I forgive? As many as seven times?" [22]Jesus said to him, "Not seven times, but, I tell you, seventy-seven times.

[23]"For this reason the kingdom of heaven may be compared to a king who wished to settle accounts with his slaves. [24]When he began the reckoning, one who owed him ten thousand talents was brought to him; [25]and, as he could not pay, his lord ordered him to be sold, together with his wife and children and all his possessions, and payment to be made.[26]So the slave fell on his knees before him, saying, 'Have patience with me, and I will pay you everything.' [27]And out of pity for him, the lord of that slave released him and forgave him the debt. [28]But that same slave, as he went out, came upon one of his fellow-slaves who owed him a hundred denarii; and seizing him by the throat, he said, 'Pay what you owe.' [29]Then his fellow-slave fell down and pleaded with him, 'Have patience with me, and I will pay you.' [30]But he refused; then he went and threw him into prison until he should pay the debt. [31]When his fellow-slaves saw what had happened, they were greatly distressed, and they went and reported to their lord all that had taken place. [32]Then his lord summoned him and said to him, 'You wicked

slave! I forgave you all that debt because you pleaded with me. [33]Should you not have had mercy on your fellow-slave, as I had mercy on you?' [34]And in anger his lord handed him over to be tortured until he should pay his entire debt.[35]So my heavenly Father will also do to every one of you, if you do not forgive your brother or sister from your heart."

## DIALOGUE 8

### *Āl 'Imrān (3):102–3*

[102]You who believe, be mindful of God, as is His due, and make sure you devote yourselves to Him, to your dying moment. [103]Hold fast to God's rope all together; do not split into factions. Remember God's favour to you: you were enemies and then He brought your hearts together and you became brothers by His grace; you were about to fall into a pit of Fire and He saved you from it—in this way God makes His revelations clear to you so that you may be rightly guided.

### *Al-Anfāl (8):61–63*

[61]But if they incline towards peace, you [Prophet] must also incline towards it, and put your trust in God: He is the All Hearing, the All Knowing. [62]If they intend to deceive you, God is enough for you: it was He who strengthened you with His help, [63]and with the believers, and brought their hearts together. Even if you had given away everything in the earth you could not have done this, but God brought them together: God is mighty and wise.

## DIALOGUE 9

### *Ephesians 2:11–22*

[11]So then, remember that at one time you Gentiles by birth, called "the uncircumcision" by those who are called "the circumcision"—a physical circumcision made in the flesh by human hands—[12]remember that you were at that time without Christ, being aliens from the commonwealth of Israel, and strangers to the covenants of promise, having no hope and without God in the world. [13]But now in Christ Jesus you who once were far off have been brought near by the blood of Christ.

[14]For he is our peace; in his flesh he has made both groups into one and has broken down the dividing wall, that is, the hostility between us. [15]He has abolished

the law with its commandments and ordinances, that he might create in himself one new humanity in place of the two, thus making peace, [16]and might reconcile both groups to God in one body through the cross, thus putting to death that hostility through it. [17]So he came and proclaimed peace to you who were far off and peace to those who were near; [18]for through him both of us have access in one Spirit to the Father. [19]So then you are no longer strangers and aliens, but you are citizens with the saints and also members of the household of God, [20]built upon the foundation of the apostles and prophets, with Christ Jesus himself as the cornerstone. [21]In him the whole structure is joined together and grows into a holy temple in the Lord; [22]in whom you also are built together spiritually into a dwelling place for God.

▲ ▲ ▲

### *Al-Ḥujurāt (49):9–13*

[9]If two groups of the believers fight, you [believers] should try to reconcile them; if one of them is [clearly] oppressing the other, fight the oppressors until they submit to God's command, then make a just and even-handed reconciliation between the two of them: God loves those who are even-handed. [10]The believers are brothers, so make peace between your two brothers and be mindful of God, so that you may be given mercy.

[11]Believers, no one group of men should jeer at another, who may after all be better than them; no one group of women should jeer at another, who may after all be better than them; do not speak ill of one another; do not use offensive nicknames for one another. How bad it is to be called a mischief-maker after accepting faith! Those who do not repent of this behaviour are evildoers. [12]Believers, avoid making too many assumptions—some assumptions are sinful—and do not spy on one another or speak ill of people behind their backs: would any of you like to eat the flesh of your dead brother? No, you would hate it. So be mindful of God: God is ever relenting, most merciful. [13]People, We created you all from a single man and a single woman, and made you into races and tribes so that you should recognize one another. In God's eyes, the most honoured of you are the ones most mindful of Him: God is all knowing, all aware.

▲ ▲ ▲

### *Al-Mumtaḥina (60):7–9*

[7]God may still bring about affection between you and your present enemies—God is all powerful, God is most forgiving and merciful—[8]and He does not for-

bid you to deal kindly and justly with anyone who has not fought you for your faith or driven you out of your homes: God loves the just. 9But God forbids you to take as allies those who have fought against you for your faith, driven you out of your homes, and helped others to drive you out: any of you who take them as allies will truly be wrongdoers.

# PART V

# Reflection

# Conversations in Virginia

LUCINDA MOSHER

**EVEN TORRENTIAL RAIN** in quantities not seen in Northern Virginia for many years could not dampen the warm fellowship and deep conversation during the thirteenth annual Building Bridges Seminar, April 27–29, 2014. While fine lectures are always a feature of these seminars, at the project's core is the lively and frank discussion encouraged by intentionally closed plenaries and the pride of place given to small-group study of a collection of preassigned texts. For Building Bridges 2014, the Airlie Center in Warrenton, Virginia, provided a picturesque and secluded venue for this work. This essay offers a brief description of the small-group process and then shares some of the highlights of Building Bridges 2014's conversations organized around this seminar's three overlapping themes: sin, forgiveness, and reconciliation. According to Building Bridges Seminar custom, the Chatham House Rule obtains: ideas shared here are unattributed; voices are quoted anonymously; quotations may actually be paraphrases. Differences between Christian and Islamic perspectives will be evident, but so will similarities. Differences among coreligionists will also be apparent.

## Small-Group Process

Building Bridges participants are assigned to one of four break-out groups, each with a preassigned moderator who encourages everyone to take a turn contributing to each discussion. These groups remain constant throughout the seminar. A session begins with a few moments of silence for gathering and centering, and then the passage(s) of scripture to be studied are read aloud. Usually, readings are of English translations. However, at the 2014 seminar one group adopted the practice of reading the assigned passage aloud in its original language first. Another group made it its custom that Bible passages be read by a Muslim, and Qur'ān passages read by a Christian. Whereas most groups had one person recite a stipulated passage in its entirety, during Building Bridges 2104 one group's practice was to proceed verse by verse, round-robin style, around the table.

However the oral reading is accomplished, once it is completed, each group member then raises up a phrase (or even a single word) that caught his or her attention, perhaps mentioning a question the phrase raised or giving a brief reason for the choice. The urge can be overwhelming at times to offer lengthy explanation or to jump in with a question immediately, but when discussion is deferred until each person has identified a compelling word or phrase, participants find the resulting theological reflection to be deeper, as interpenetrating themes emerge.

## Sin

For one group, comparing the biblical and Qur'ānic accounts of Adam and Eve raised questions regarding human vicegerency. Among Islamic scholars, one Muslim explained, two interpretations may be found: "Some say that vicegerency is given to Adam and Eve only; others say that vicegerency is given to all human beings." The scriptural teaching that God created human beings who then nearly immediately sinned raised questions about theodicy: How does a good God permit evil? "We humans have a need for explanation," one Christian noted. "Theology is a human activity, and it is a limited activity. Julian of Norwich distinguished between what we humans see in our sight and how God sees things. We are invited to trust, not to expect an explanation."

A Muslim, referring to *The Conference of the Birds* by Farīd ud-Dīn ʿAṭṭār, said that Adam had become too attached to paradise. In being sent away to Earth, he was, in actuality, restored to closeness to God. Another Muslim concurred: "God has a plan, but Adam and Eve did not know it. God knew the capacity of human beings." He noted further that paradise in the Adam and Eve story is not necessarily identical to the Garden of the Hereafter. With regard to human vicegerency, another Muslim asserted, "God had always intended Adam to be on Earth; it was not a punishment. Being on Earth is something to be grateful for."

According to the Qur'ān, a Christian observed, Adam already has the religion of humanity, whereas in Christianity the religion of humankind comes with Abraham. "What is the religion of Adam? We don't have details," replied a Muslim. "Perhaps it is 'natural religion.'"

Hearing Romans 5:11–21 and Genesis 3:1–24 read in succession provoked questions about double predestination from a Catholic at the table. "Lutherans are not Calvinists!" another Christian responded. "Luther thought he taught the perfection of Catholic thought." The exchange continued. "What about people who appear to be in rejection of everything God wants? If their rejection is on their own, then they are more powerful than God! This cannot be. Thus, God must have ordained their reprobation! Can that be? We cannot know. So it comes down to trust and grace. In light of God's glory, we can only see how glory and grace cooperate."

"Calvinists had the same instinct to root grace in the eternal will of God," a Christian clarified. "Reprobation must be willed by God, they would say, because grace is irresistible." From a Lutheran point of view, he continued, "one can, as a sinner, feel justified—but one still has one's sins! After a process of lifelong learning, in the end our sins no longer accuse us. From a Reformed point of view, we *know* we are on the right side. The evidence? Our life flourishes! This is a happy, but not deep, understanding."

When read through a Muslim lens, Romans 5 raised questions about describing God in human terms: "Does anthropomorphism delimit God's power?" Paul is spinning an extended metaphor here, answered one Christian. Another concurred, saying that in religious texts "the metaphorical and the literal dimensions often overlap."

A Muslim asked for clarification about Genesis 3:16. "It implies the double punishment of women," he noted. "Also, the Qur'ān does not 'name' the tree from which Adam and Eve eat." In the biblical account, a Christian explained, "God starts with a permission: it is all right to eat from *all* the trees. Then God adds a prohibition: except this one! There is no curse on Adam and Eve, only on the serpent. In saying, 'Go forth and procreate,' God is saying that humanity has a future!" A Muslim woman brought up "a common belief among Muslim women that women's sins are forgiven when in labor: during labor their supplications are accepted."

Another important lesson of Genesis 3:16, said one Christian, is that sinning does not happen in isolation. It is not quite fair to say that "Christians have Original Sin, whereas Muslims have Personal Responsibility." A Muslim replied that the consequence of sin is twofold: personal and existential. "If we compare the biblical and Qur'ānic accounts, we'll see that the Qur'ān has no special role for Eve." A Christian noted that Paul does not take up Eve either: "He sticks to Adam."

A common theme of popular preaching, one Christian noted, "is that 'work' is the price we pay for sin. But theology also seeks a positive role for work. Interpretations of Genesis 3 are often deeply contextual, reflecting social attitudes of the time."

In considering al-Aʿrāf (7):10–27, one Christian was intrigued by the degree to which "shame" comes up in the passage. Another wondered whether the "original sin" was Iblīs's. (Iblīs's insistence that he is better than Adam leads to disobedience.) Another noted the tension in the Qur'ān's lesson that God has placed human beings on Earth with the authority of vicegerency, yet the sending down is also punishment. "'Original Sin' is a technical term," a Muslim rebutted. "It would be better to say that this is the first moment of sinfulness."

Particularly fascinating to one group was the conversation between Iblīs and God in al-A'rāf (7):10–27. "Iblīs can argue with God!" one participant exclaimed. "He brings options to the table!" A Christian wondered whether arguing with God is part of Islamic spirituality; is *complaint* part of Muslim prayer? A Muslim answered, "The Qur'ān tells us *not* to argue with God, and yet here Iblīs is doing just that!" Another Muslim added, "Yes, complaint, but not arguing, since total submission is required. We are taught that there is good for us in the unpleasant things." In the second part of his dialogue with God, Iblīs says what he is going to do to Adam and Eve. "This seems a bit like the beginning of the biblical story of Job," a Christian noted. "There, Satan is given divine permission to test Job."

In fact, for more than one group, the sin of Adam versus the sin of Iblīs was a major focus of conversation. Pride is the sin for Iblīs in the Qur'ān and for Adam and Eve in the Bible. One group sought to differentiate between "mistakes" and "sins"—"slips" versus intentional disobedience. "Sin goes deeper than the doing of wrong actions," one Christian asserted. In another group a Muslim noted how, in some Christian circles, "a very masculine, patriarchal reading of Genesis is now being balanced by feminist readings. The same thing is happening in Islam."

During a session devoted to study of Romans 7:14–25 in conversation with al-A'rāf (7):177–79 and Yūsuf (12):18 and 58, one Muslim observed that, according to the Qur'ān, sin prevents the body from functioning as it should. A Christian participant agreed: "The Qur'ān's diagnosis of the human condition is that humans are 'heedless'; they forget!"

Al-A'rāf (7):179 provoked considerable discussion of free will versus predestination to hell. Someone suggested that God could be speaking ironically here. Another noted that the Qur'ān says repeatedly that God did not create in jest. The Qur'ān says that God knows what we do not know. God knows the risk in creation. Another asserted that his fellow Muslims would be willing to say that we humans cannot second-guess God.

Turning to Romans 7, one Christian explained that Paul is not engaging in a moral critique of sin here; rather, "slavery" is one of Paul's main metaphors for sin. Another concurred, noting that in this text, "sin" is a personified power. A Muslim noted that the Qur'ān speaks of a "deceiver." But Satan insists that he does not "make" people sin; rather, he just calls and we answer! A Christian observed that from a Qur'ānic perspective every act by its very being requires God's action. Humans *acquire* ownership of the action. In this the Asharite emphasis is even stronger than that of Augustine or the Calvinists. Some agency must be subscribed to humans, but God's sovereignty must be preserved. The Qur'ān plays up God's sovereignty and plays down human agency. For example, in the Annunciation, the Qur'ān does not record Mary's response, whereas the Gospel of Luke does. A Muslim added that the Qur'ān is always trying to maintain the tension between questions of divine sovereignty and human agency, leaving it irresolvable.

In summarizing, one group explored differences in the ways sin is characterized. Another group observed that in both the Christian and the Islamic tradition, sin is something that God *can* use for something good. Another group reported its discovery of "a common, overwhelming sense of God's mercy—albeit expressed differently. Sin can be a portal for experiencing God's grace," the members said. Thus, a day devoted to the study of "sin" had not been bleak.

## Forgiveness

What is the cost of forgiveness? From Christian and Muslim perspectives, what does forgiveness involve? In considering the parable of the prodigal son (Luke 15:11–32), one Christian insisted that it is not to be read as an "example" story. "We need to distinguish between what *God* can do and what *we* can do." In Matthew 18:21–35, when Peter asks how often a community member who sins against him should be forgiven, Jesus tells a parable about the high price of failing to forgive. "The enablement of one's ability to forgive is entirely God's doing," the Christian participant continued. "What does it cost *us* to forgive? We have to say 'yes' to the pain inflicted on us. And forgiveness can also be costly to the one forgiven!"

After a Muslim had read the parable of the prodigal son to his group, one Christian offered that Luke's text "tells us how God is, but also lifts up a standard of perfection for us." A Muslim responded, "What the father says to the older son is also fascinating: 'You think what I can give is finite. Actually, I have infinite love, infinite wealth to give!' It's about human zero-sum game versus God's prodigality, God's endless abundance."

Another Muslim suggested that there are two types of forgiveness: one has to do with remembering rightly; the other, with forgetting. "The Qur'ān offers a notion of forgiveness as 'covering the sin'—which is parallel to the lesson of the prodigal son; it also offers a notion of 'erasing the sin.'"

"All of us are the younger son in this story," one Christian asserted. "Indeed, a Muslim agreed, "this is a successful story because we can all relate to it! I can see parallels in it to the Prophet's behavior. The young son's intention is there; so, even before he can speak, his request has been fulfilled." Another Muslim concurred:

"God is never going to fail God's servants, no matter how you see the distribution of resources in this world." This remark caused a Christian to recall the biblical parable of the day laborers who all got the same pay—no matter how many hours they worked. A Muslim found it intriguing: "Why do we get angry about the good fortune of others?" he mused. "We compare and despair!"

"How about the process of forgiveness itself?" asked a Muslim. "Love God, love your neighbor as yourself," a Christian replied. "Augustine rightly points out that self-love is necessary." But what does it mean to properly love oneself? Before this group could settle on an answer, a Muslim returned the members' attention to the younger son in the parable: "He's going through a rough time, but when he decides to return home and ask his father for mercy, has he really changed? Is he being repentant or expedient?" Pointing to Luke 15:17, a Christian noted, "The text says that the young man 'went inside himself.' He took a look inside himself. That might indicate some real change." And a Muslim noted, "The ability of the father to accept the son back is part of the healing process."

What if, wondered a Christian, rather than being a Bible story, the parable of the prodigal son were a freestanding tale? "In the Gospel of Luke, it is told by Jesus, but could Muḥammad have told this story?" Opinions in this group were many. The reference, in Luke 15:25, to celebratory music and dancing sparked a lively discussion of the range of Muslim attitudes toward music and dance—thus appropriate ways for Muslims to express happiness. But one Muslim was more interested in "jealousy" as a theme in this parable. "It is also an important theme in Sūra Yūsuf," she pointed out. "Jealousy is a 'heart disease.' The Qur'ān and the Sunnah admonish against favoring one son over another (or one wife over another)," she explained. "But Muḥammad had his favorites," countered another Muslim. "And Jesus had an inner circle of three disciples," a Christian offered. "Yet," said another Christian, bringing this discussion to a close, "as Dante said, 'We're all petals of the same rose.'"

For one group, discussion of forgiveness was intertwined with respective understandings of confession. One Muslim recalled a ḥadīth his parents had stressed throughout his childhood: God is more joyful to receive a repentant sinner than is a man who has lost a camel in the desert and receives it back! "Yes," he stressed, "there still is emphasis on justice. People on the straight path must be kept alert! Yet for those who are 'astray,' there is always hope."

Another Muslim said that from an Islamic perspective forgiveness is active. "The Prophet turned to God seventy times a day, even though his sins were forgiven. One is to be a grateful servant." She wondered, is the Christian perspective on forgiveness more passive? "In some streams of Christianity," one Christian replied, "forgiveness has sacramental aspects. Some Christians practice regular confession of sins to a priest. Thus, there is a regular giving of an account of your own sinfulness and asking forgiveness." In Christianity, another Christian added, "sin is understood as fracturing one's relationship with God; it is 'harming' or offending God. From a Protestant point of view, nothing I could do could repair this fracture; there must be divine initiative or motion." Christians may speak of the assurance of divine grace, he continued; "but Roman Catholics and Lutherans disagree as to whether assurance of grace guarantees pardon."

Citing al-Ghazālī and al-Nawawi, a Muslim noted that according to Islamic scholars, "there is a four-step process of repentance: feel remorse; ask God's forgiveness; make amends, if possible; and promise sincerely never to do this sinful thing again." She wondered whether there is a process of repentance for Christians. "The four steps you've outlined are almost identical to the preparation for Roman Catholic confession," a Christian responded. There ensued a lengthy discussion of various Christian practices of formal confession and of confession as recollection of baptism.

Another Muslim mentioned the transactional nature of Islam: in the end, Muslims hope to have a big enough account of good deeds. "Backsliding is no problem for God," he noted. "God will forgive again. Re-sinning and asking for forgiveness again is better than righteous behavior that leads to arrogance." If Islam is transactional, "then what is the currency?" a Christian asked. "Who forgives, and who communicates forgiveness?" In Islam, a Muslim replied, "only God forgives. The Prophet Muḥammad could express God's forgiveness." Another Muslim clarified: "The language is transactional, but the ḥadīth is clear that we enter heaven via God's mercy. In the Day of Judgment, those who were oppressed will enter ahead of the others." The first Muslim agreed: "God says, 'I will not forgive the person who violates the rights of another.'"

In their conversation on Romans 8:1–4, one group considered the difference between law as Sharīʿa (which enables us to reach God) and law as *nomos* (which acts as a mirror to show us our brokenness and our inability to reach God on our own). "In Jesus Christ we have another mirror," a Christian noted. "It reflects that it is *his* grace that enables us to reach perfection. We need to be forgiven first, so that we can go on to fulfill the law." Continuing on the notion of the law as a mirror and as a means to find one's identity as people of God, another Christian explained, "When we are brought into Christ, we are brought into new relation with the law." From here this group considered various Protestant and Jewish understandings of "law" and the good things that the law has as object.

"Christian tradition differentiates between *justification* and *sanctification*," one Christian pointed out. "Sanctification comes *after* the moment of God's work." In fact, another Christian continued, Paul's Epistle to the Romans "is about living a forgiven life. We are given the gift of the Holy Spirit dwelling in us. It is about participation in Christ. Christ took up the law, died, rose. We participate in this through baptism into the dying and rising."

So, said a Muslim, "we have a Muslim and a Christian together on a street, each doing good work. One is striving toward forgiveness. The other is thanking God for what has already been received." Another Muslim nodded. "Dos and don'ts are very strong in Islam. We are to be disciplined, preparing for the day when we'll be in the presence of the divine. It seems as if Christians have it easy." A Christian countered, "I think we're agreed on God's guiding our good behavior. The problem is *the Cross!* It is a scandal, a point of real difference. We disagreed on whether it happened, on whether it was needed." An ancient Christian prayer, noted one Christian, says that "one of the Trinity was crucified for us." Picking up on this, another Christian explained that in Jesus's crucifixion, "God was not laying on someone the sins of someone else. Rather, God was bearing the sins of others himself."

"Under the law," yet another Christian said, "the word of God spoken in the word is condemned to die. God has borne that: the law as humans have twisted it. Law observance makes self-righteousness—which makes us persecute. The Cross shows what damage law can do. If you are 'in Christ Jesus,' you allow yourself to be drawn into what God has made available. Paul found himself to be completely condemned. His story teaches us that God comes and finds us."

From this comment arose a lengthy discussion of grace. "In both traditions, there is a relationship between grace and action," a Muslim pointed out. "In each tradition there is a safety net. There is grace you hope for; there is grace you work for!" Indeed, he continued, "the Qur'ān includes many verses about immediate exchange of good deeds for bad, many verses about being a Friend of God. This is 'Good News.'" Pointing to Hūd (11):106–8, he asserted, "the Christian explanation of grace makes sense according to its founder; the Muslim explanation of grace also makes sense." And, said a Christian in response, "we are trying to answer slightly different questions."

## Reconciliation

In the seminar's opening plenary, Veli-Matti Kärkkäinen explained that reconciliation begins with learning how to "remember rightly."[1] In a later session the seminar considered the link between reconciliation and peacemaking. One Muslim asked whether justice and reconciliation are incompatible. "I am fascinated by the notion of host and guest. The measure of justice lies in how you treat your guest. Is this also the measure of reconciliation?" "Justice is a polyvalent term," a Christian replied. "We often assume it is legal—all punishment. Is there a way justice can be seen as *embracing* reconciliation? Need they be opposites?" When the Qur'ān speaks of reconciliation, another Muslim pointed out, "there is no stress on deciding who is right and wrong. Rather the two simply embrace each other. There is no simple definition of justice. Is it always about a settling of claims? No; it can also be restoration."

The notion of settling claims was at the core of the parable of the unforgiving servant (Matt. 18:21–35). "We read that text in liturgy," noted one Christian, "then we say, 'Thanks be to God'; but are we thankful for this text?" This is indeed a difficult parable, many agreed. "In it there is the human expectation of God to forgive," one Muslim observed, "which then comes up against God's expectation that we are to forgive each other. We need to see God in human beings." Another Muslim nodded: "Do unto other as you would have done to you. I wonder: if in this parable the king stands for God, did God really forgive the debt? The debt was reinstated. What about 'forgive and forget'?"

"This story is repulsive," a Christian agreed, "but somewhere, someone is doing this [what we see happening in this story] to someone. It is a reminder of the need for compassion and solidarity." Another Christian saw this story as illustrating a "failure to understand the relation between the horizontal and the vertical. The forgiveness was never truly received!" Another Christian concurred: "The parable's point is that the servant's heart has not been penetrated by the extravagant generosity of God. To harden your heart against God is to risk destroying yourself! I have no difficulty in applying this to myself! If I hold a hard heart, ultimately it will destroy me. But accepting forgiveness is always hard." Indeed, a Muslim agreed, "God can give abundantly, but the human condition is hard! The debt is wiped, but the slave still needs money!"

"Threats don't enable me to move out and be more forgiving," one Christian said. "The punishment imagery in this parable overwhelms me." Another Christian agreed that it is possible to inflate the contrast so much that the meaning is lost. "Remember what's actually happening in this story: he who was forgiven *much* refuses to forgive even *a little*." "Jesus encourages us to see how much we've been given in him," a third Christian noted. "I need to remember just how much I've been forgiven."

A Muslim countered, "From an Islamic viewpoint, how do I know I have been forgiven? The premise of this story doesn't work for me as a Muslim." A central notion of Islamic theology, another Muslim responded, is that hope and fear work together: don't despair, but don't be presumptuous, don't be too sure."

"One has to be taken over by the confidence of what one has received," a Christian pointed out. "Baptism gives you a new ontology," said another; "it makes you part of the Body of Christ—but you then have to *work with* that!" "From an Islamic point of view," a Muslim added, "there is the question of whether one's good deeds will be received. One way to find out is to see the consequences in your life. If there is no self-transformation, then probably your good deeds were not accepted." A second Christian noted how often his coreligionists say, "You can't forgive others until you forgive yourself." Perhaps that is compatible with the parable of the unforgiving servant, he suggested: "It's easy to say, 'Don't be self-obsessed.' But for a person caught in a circle of obsession, that won't help." "But it is the community that is therapeutic," the first Christian replied; "healing comes in relationship to other people." "What strikes me," said her interlocutor, bringing the discussion of Matthew 18 to a close, "is that the whole community of Jesus's disciples abandons him. The whole community is reconstituted by God in resurrection. Jesus takes them back! *That* is empowering! This parable is *not* empowering."

Harking back to the previous day's engagement with the parable of the prodigal son, a Muslim noted that—in that story—"the father's generosity does not bring reconciliation. Rather, it increases resentment on the part of the older brother; it thwarts justice. Forgiveness without justice can thwart reconciliation." However, the Christian replied, an interesting element of that parable is that "the narrative is left suspended. Much is left to the listener. We are left to decide where *we* are in the story, to confront our own dysfunction."

"Note the contrast," another Christian urged, "between distributive and restorative justice on the one hand, and eschatological justice on the other. In the end, even the dead are raised! What is unjust in the old order might be just in the future. There may be harmony in spite of the past. What is the *aim* of reconciliation? We should all be one, but what *kind* of oneness are we seeking? A oneness that allows for difference? Can we say, 'I want the other to be part of my future?' If so, the other remains 'other.' This is an implication for Eucharist. Drawing-room communitarianism smooths things over, whereas radical hospitality allows the other to be 'other.'" Muḥammad ʿAbduh said as much, one of the Muslims pointed out; there could be "differences" while living together in a just state.

As one group dug deeply into al-Anfāl (8):61–63, a Muslim noted that verse 61 ("if they incline toward peace, you must also incline toward it") is a conditional sentence: "sometimes fighting is okay." Pointing to verse 62 ("If they intend to deceive you, God is enough for you"), another Muslim said, "What fascinates me about the Qur'ān is that it is addressed over time to a community that goes through various crises. At times, they're not to fight back; at other times, they're told it is OK to fight back. The Qur'ān is like the letters of Paul in this way, in that both are addressing community situations."

One of the Qur'ānic verses assigned for study, Āl ʿImrān (3):102 ("You who believe, be mindful of God, as is His due, and make sure you devote yourselves to Him, to your dying moment"), is said by Muslims at every Jumah, a Muslim explained to his discussion group. "All Islamic legal schools agree that for a *khut-*

*bah* [sermon] to be valid, you must remember your death. The easiest way to do that is to recite Āl ʿImrān (3):102." In response a Christian noted, "One of the most common Roman Catholic prayers, the Hail Mary, includes the line 'Remember us now and at the hour of our death.' To die a good death is to live well." A Muslim asked her, "Is there some sort of notion of reconciliation that ritualizes 'death' and reawakening? Die before you die; awaken to truth; set aside petty differences." "Baptism does this," she replied. "Are there ritualized reconciliations?" the Muslim pressed. A Christian mentioned ways in which "reconciliation" is part of what happens in every Eucharist. Another mentioned the sacrament of the Reconciliation of a Penitent. Another noted that some Christians even practice a "baptism of backsliders."

Turning to al-Mumtaḥina (60):7–9, one Muslim called it foundational for conducting international relations. "According to this verse, a believer can expect five rights or duties from another believer." A Christian noted how the passage "moves from promise (in verse 7) to permission (in verse 8) to prescription (in verse 9). It is an example of how a reconciling act of God can provide a new basis for relationship. It enables us to behave in a particular way." A Muslim noted that verse 9 applies while a conflict rages; "there are other verses that apply to situations once the conflict has ceased. One ḥadīth says, 'Do not ask God for war; but, if it comes, then stand your ground.'" This verse is an example of a "prescription," a Christian noted, and prescriptions function differently from narratives. "In ethics, a narrative can illustrate good behavior."

"What is the role of Jesus," asked one Muslim, "in reconciling humans to God? If you believe, does that transform you, and does that then reconcile you?" How is it different from Muslim notions of reconciliation? "When one accepts Jesus," one Christian offered, "one accepts his forgiveness. It is a hypostatic union, a complete wedding of humanity and divinity. However, if there is no outworking of the faith, there is no faith in the first place! One cannot turn to God without turning to humanity."

"What about the salvation of non-Christians?" a Muslim asked. "That depends on your starting point," a Christian responded. "Luther would have said that Muslims don't know properly how God relates to humanity." Another Christian noted that Matthew 25, the parable of the Last Judgment, "is nicely ambiguous." Interestingly, noted one Christian, referring to Romans 7, Paul is both slightly universalistic and slightly predestinarian: God allowed all to sin so that God could save all.

For Qurʾānic hints of universalism, the group was reminded, look at al-Anʿām (6):128: "'Your home is the Fire, and there you shall remain'—unless God wills otherwise." "The great scholar Ibn Taymiyyah saw in this verse a mitigation of *all* divine threats," one Muslim noted. In other places the Qurʾān speaks of punishment for "a long time." One can argue that "a long time" is not the same as "forever." Some Muslim scholars argue that divine redemption of human beings happens *within* Hell.

## Conclusion

As Building Bridges 2014 drew to a close, questions remained about the intrinsic nature of reconciliation. What *do* we mean by "unity"? Is it practical? Is it possible? What is the difference between *unity* and *consensus*? Between *agreement* and *consensus*? Questions of the salvation of nonbelievers are "vertical axis" issues, matters of the divine–human reconciliation; Christians and Muslims do not always agree among themselves on these issues—let alone with each other. With regard to the horizontal axis, human-to-human reconciliation, Christian and Muslim attitudes and ideas are remarkably similar, one participant noted. And as the group had agreed, another asserted, "that reconciliation cannot be commanded." Interestingly, one Christian observed, when discussing forgiveness, the theological differences between the traditions seemed significant. But with regard to reconciliation, significant similarities had been seen. Further, the need for intrafaith reconciliation is clear. In any case, as one Muslim summarized, "reconciliation is not sameness; rather, it is agreement that there are indeed two points of view. It is a celebration, not the obliteration, of differences."

Given the strife in certain parts of the world today, one Christian stressed, "reconciliation is an urgent need! People demand that we theologians talk about reconciliation—but we're not to mention 'religion' because dogma is seen as the source of the problems! The main cause of the problem cannot be the fountain of the solution." A Muslim responded, "It depends on what we mean by 'religion.' We are also challenged to rethink our texts. New readings of certain verses are being promulgated. There has indeed been attrition in religious authority, but 'religion' *can* be part of the solution." "Religion, politics, and more get blended together in decidedly unhelpful ways," said one Christian; "each can be deeply divisive, when they are meant to symbolize unity. We misuse religion!" "Religion is like fire," a Muslim suggested; "it provides warmth, but can also wreak destruction."

For Building Bridges 2014 participants, what was the best part of dialogical study of sacred texts? "We read each other's scripture!" one Muslim answered, "and a Christian read the Qur'ān really beautifully!" Another Muslim wondered whether Christians have a practice equivalent to the *basmala*: the Muslim custom of reciting "In the Name of God, most Compassionate, most Merciful" when beginning to read scripture. There are indeed similar practices, said one Christian, but they are not universal. Much depends on context. During Building Bridges Seminars, a Christian suggested, Psalm 19:14 could be adapted to this purpose: "May the words of my mouth and the meditation of my heart be acceptable to you, O LORD, my rock and my redeemer."

In reflecting on the scripture-dialogue experience, it was clear that while break-out groups were free to allow their conversation to flow in any direction it might, most had stayed close to the assigned texts during their discussions. As this report should reveal, engagement was earnest; delicate matters and differences of opinion were not avoided. "What began to emerge from our conversations," one participant asserted, "was an awareness of deep similarity between our traditions."

## Note

1 Veli-Matti Kärkkäinen, "Sin, Forgiveness, and Reconciliation: A Christian Perspective," p. 9 in this volume.

# INDEX

ʿAbduh, Muḥammad, 44–45, 50–54, 57, 61, 64n68, 110, 112
Abel, 37n5
Abelard, Peter, 6
Abraham, 102, 126
Absalom, 8
accommodation, 97–98
Adam and Eve: in Bible, 4, 18, 25–26, 27–29, 67–69, 127; in Qurʾān, 42–44, 69–71, 128; in *tafsīr*, 44–54. *See also* Eden; Fall
agreement, 136
ʿAlī, Yūsuf, 65n93
ʿAlī ibn Abī Ṭālib, 41–42
angels, 43, 45–46, 54–56, 62n22
Anglicanism, 4
Anselm of Canterbury, 6, 10n3, 12n19
anthropomorphism, 127
*aphesis*, 7
*aphiemi*, 7
Aquinas, 10n3, 32–33, 38n10, 38n14
arbitration, 97
Ashʿarism, 65n80, 128–29
atonement, 6
ʿAṭṭār, Farīd ud-Dīn, 126
Augustine, 4, 10n3, 11n7, 31–32, 35, 130
Ayoub, Mahmoud, 63n29

Banchoff, Thomas, xiv
baptism, 12n19, 30, 133
Baqara, al-, 42, 46, 47, 49–50, 57, 60
Barth, Karl, 31, 35
belief, 57–58
Ben Sira, 76–77
Bible: forgiveness in, 6–7, 8, 12n17, 90–91, 92; reconciliation in, 98–100, 102, 118–19; sin in, 24–25, 66–69, 70; version used, xiv. *See also* Christianity; Judaism
*Bondage of the Will, The* (Luther), 4
Brown, Richard, xv
Building Bridges Seminar, xi, 125–26

Cain, 37n5
Calvin, John, 80
Calvinism, 126–27
Catholicism. *See* Roman Catholicism
*charis*, 82
Chatham House Rule, 125
Christianity: Fall in, in Western vs. Eastern thinking, 3–4; forgiveness in, 6–10, 11n13, 75–82; reconciliation in, 6–10, 97–105; sin in, 3, 5. *See also* Bible; Jesus Christ
Codina, Victor, 104
conciliation, 97
condemnation, 9
*Conference of the Birds, The* (ʿAṭṭār), 126
creation, 27, 43, 48–49, 52

David, 8, 17
death, 5–6, 26
DeGioia, John J., xi, xiv
desire, 28
devil, 27–28, 43, 44–48, 49, 52, 54, 56, 62n22, 86–87, 128

*dhanb*, 40, 41, 61n2
disobedience, 40, 47–48
divisiveness, 109
"double predestination," 4, 126–27

Eastern Orthodox Church, 3
eating together, 104
ecumenism, 99
Eden, 26–29, 43, 49–50, 52–53
embrace, 8
Ephesians, 99–100, 119–20
Erasmus of Rotterdam, 4
Eucharist, 103–5
evil, 14, 23–24, 27, 38n14, 40–41, 52–54, 59–60
evolution, 5
exclusion, 8

*fāḥisha*, 41
Fall: in ʿAbduh, 50–54; in al-Rāzī, 48–50; in al-Ṭabarī, 44–48; in Bible, 67–69; death and, 5–6; in Eastern Orthodox Church, 3; interpretations of, across Abrahamic religions, 3; in Islam, 18; in Judaism, 3, 10n2; in Qurʾān, 43–44, 46–48, 69–71; in *tafsīr*, 44–54. *See also* Adam and Eve; Eden
First Testament, 8
forgiveness: in al-Ghazālī, 85; among humans, 8–10; atonement and, 6; in Bible, 6–7, 8, 12n17, 90–91, 92, 98–99; in Building Bridges Seminar, 129–32; in Christianity, 6–10, 11n13, 12n17, 75–82; condemnation and, 9; divine, 6–7; economic aspect of, 78; in Ephesians, 99–100; example of, 13–14; generosity of, 7; as gift, 82; God and, 6, 8, 14, 78–79, 87–88; in ḥadīth, 84–85; in Islam, 11n13, 13–14, 83–88; Jesus Christ and, 6–7, 9, 79; in Judaism, 7; justice and, 9, 14–15; in Lord's Prayer, 98–99; in Luke, 75–79, 90–91; in Matthew, 98–99; mercy and, 7, 15, 17–18; of neighbor, 8; in Paul, 76, 80–81, 131–32; in Qurʾān, 91–94; reconciliation and, 9–10; redemption and, 75–76, 79–82; repentance and, 7, 12n19, 77–78, 84–86; resentment and, 8–9; in Riḍā, 85–86; in Romans, 80–81, 92; as sacrament, 130–31; *shirk* and, 85–86; unconditional, 7
formalism, 16–17
freedom, 4, 56–57, 128
*Freedom of the Will, The* (Erasmus of Rotterdam), 4

Garden of Eden, 26–29, 43, 49–50, 52–53. *See also* Adam and Eve; Fall
generosity, of forgiveness, 7
Ghazālī, Abū Ḥāmid al-, 58–59, 60, 85, 131
God: anthropomorphization of, 127; devil and, 52; forgiveness and, 6, 8, 14, 78–79, 87–88; mercy of, 15; reconciliation and, 101; sin and, 25, 28, 33–34, 41
Good Samaritan, 102
grace, 82, 110, 127

*ḥadd*, 41
ḥadīth: creation in, 53; forgiveness in, 84–85
heart, 58–59, 107
hospitality, 101–5
*ḥudūd*, 41

Iblīs, 44–48, 49, 52, 54, 56, 62n22, 128. *See also* devil
Ibn ʿAbbās, 42, 46
Ibn al-ʿArabī, 85, 86, 87
Ibn Ḥanbal, Aḥmad, 44
Ibn Isḥāq, 47, 108–9
Ibn Kathīr, 109–10
Ibn Masʿūd, ʿAbd Allāh, 41, 46
Ibn Taymitta, 86
Ibn Taymiyyah, 135–36
Ibn Ubayy, ʿAbd Allāh, 88
Ibn ʿUmar, 42
International Ecumenical Peace Convention, 10
*Introduction to Christianity* (Kierkegaard), 23
Irenaeus, 6

Islam: belief in, 57–58; devil in, 44–46; Fall in, 3, 18; forgiveness in, 11n13, 13–14, 83–88; freedom in, 56–57; judgment in, 14, 15–16; justice in, 14–15; mercy in, 17–18; murder in, 13; non-Muslims in, 17; predestination in, 18; prophets in, 42, 49, 50, 54–56, 59, 85; reconciliation in, 107–16; repentance in, 84–86; salvation in, 86–88; *shirk* in, 85–86; sin in, 14–17, 18, 40–61. *See also* ḥadīth; Muḥammad; Qurʾān
*ʿiṣyān*, 40, 61n1
*ithm*, 40, 41, 61n2

Jawziyya, Ibn Qayyim al-, 86
Jesus Christ: forgiveness and, 6–7, 9, 79; hospitality and, 102; reconciliation and, 99–100; resurrection of, 30; sin and, 24–25. *See also* Christianity
Jewett, Paul, 5
jinn, 44–45
John, 25
John the Baptist, 7
Joseph, 8, 59
Jubāʾī, Abū ʿAlī al-, 65n80
Judaism: Fall in, 3, 10n1; forgiveness in, 7
judgment: Fall and, 3, 29; in Islam, 14, 15–16; reconciliation and, 102–3; sin and, 14, 15–16, 29, 35–36
justice, 9, 12n19, 14–15, 32, 132–33, 134

*kabīra*, 41
Kharijites, 55, 58
*khaṭīʾa*, 40, 41, 61n2
Kierkegaard, Søren, 23

Last Supper, 104
Leppin, Volker, 37n10
Lord's Prayer, 98–99
Luke, 7, 75–79, 90–91, 102
Luther, Martin, 4, 33, 35–36
Lutheranism, 126–27

Madigan, Daniel, xi, xiv
Mark, 7
Marshall, David, xiv, 10n1
*maʿṣiya*, 40, 41, 61n1
Matthew, 98–99, 118–19
Māturīdī, Abū Manṣūr al-, 53
Maximus the Confessor, 9
mercy, 7, 15, 17–18, 84
Moral Example, 6
moralism, 23
Moses, 8, 18
Muḥammad: murder in teachings of, 13; reconciliation and, 108–9. *See also* Islam; Qurʾān
murder, 13–14. *See also* sin
Musekura, Celestin, 9–10
Muʿtazilites, 55–56, 57, 64n75, 65n80

*nafs*, 58–60
nakedness, 47
neighbor, forgiveness of, 8
Neoplatonism, 31
New Testament: forgiveness in, 75–76; reconciliation in, 98–100, 102; sin in, 24–25. *See also* Bible; Paul
Nicene-Constantinopolitan Creed, 7
Niebuhr, R., 4
nudity, 47

original sin, 3–4, 18, 27–29, 127–28. *See also* sin

Paradise, 5
Paul, 4, 7, 25–26, 26–27, 29–30, 70, 76, 80–81, 100–101, 128, 131–32
Pelagius, 31–32
Penal Substitution, 6
Peter, 104, 129
power, 77
predestination, 4, 18, 126–27
prodigal son, 129, 130
prophets, in Islam, 42, 49, 50, 54–56, 59, 85
Protestantism, 4, 6, 98
Psalms, 24

Qurʾān: Adam and Eve in, 42–44, 69–71, 128; angels in, 46, 54–56, 62n22; devil in, 43, 47, 49, 54, 56, 62n22; Fall in,

43–44, 46–48, 69–71; forgiveness in, 91–94; garden in, 49–50, 52–53; judgment in, 15–16; mercy in, 15, 17–18; murder in, 13; non-Muslims in, 17; reconciliation in, 16–17, 107–16, 119, 120–21; sin in, 40–61, 61n4, 69–71; success in, 83–84; translation of, xiv. *See also* ḥadīth; Islam; Muḥammad; *tafsīr*
Qurṭubī, al-, 109, 113

Rāzī, Fakhr al-Dīn al-, 44–45, 48–50, 54–56, 60, 63n26, 113, 115
reconciliation, 136; in ʿAbduh, 110, 112; accommodation vs., 97–98; in al-Qurṭubī, 109, 113; in al-Ṭabarī, 108–9, 111–13, 114; in al-Zamakhsharī, 114–15; in Bible, 98–100, 118–19, 119–20; in Building Bridges Seminar, 132–36; in Christianity, 6–10, 97–105; eating together and, 104; in Ephesians, 99–100, 119–20; Eucharist and, 103–5; example of, 13–14; God and, 101; hospitality and, 101–5; in Ibn Kathīr, 109–10; in Islam, 107–16; Jesus Christ and, 99–100; judgment and, 102–3; justice and, 132–33, 134; in Matthew, 98–99, 118–19; meaning of, 97–98; mercy and, 17–18; in Old Testament, 102; in Paul, 100–101; in Qurʾān, 16–17, 107–16, 119–20; in Rāzī, 113, 115; Rule of Saint Benedict and, 103; tolerance vs., 97–98
redemption, 75–76, 79–82
Reformers, 38n14, 39n18
repentance, 7, 12n19, 77–78, 84–86
resentment, 8–9
resurrection, 30
revelation, 23
revenge, 9
Riḍā, Muḥammad Rashīd, 44–45, 51–53, 85–86
Roman Catholicism, 4, 98
Rule of Saint Benedict, 103

*ṣaghīra*, 41
salvation, 75, 86–88
Samaritans, 102
sanctification, 131–32
Satan, 27–28, 43, 44–48, 49, 52, 54, 86–87
Satisfaction, 6
*sayyiʾa*, 40, 41
science, 5
self-love, 130
serpent, 27–28. *See also* devil; Iblīs
"sharing the table," 104
Sharīʿa: murder in, 13
*sharr*, 40–41
*shirk*, 85–86
sin: in ʿAbduh, 50–54; across Abrahamic religions, 3; in al-Ghazālī, 58–59; in al-Rāzī, 48–50, 54–56; in al-Ṭabarī, 44–48; in Aquinas, 32–33, 38n10, 38n14; in Augustine, 31–32, 35; belief and, 57–58; in Bible, 24–25, 66–69, 70; in Building Bridges Seminar, 126–29; changing meanings of, 23; Christ and, 24–25; in Christianity, 5; death and, 5–6, 26; disambiguation of, 40–42; as dislocation, 34–35; doctrinal debates over, 31–34; Eden and, 26–29; God and, 25, 28, 33–34, 41; inevitability of, 29–30; in Islam, 14–17, 18, 40–61; in John, 25; judgment and, 15–16, 29, 35–36; in Kierkegaard, 23; in Luther, 33, 35–36; major vs. minor, 41–42; mercy and, 15; in New Testament, 24–25; in Old Testament, 24; original, 3–4, 18, 27–29, 127–28; overcoming of, 29–30; in Paul, 25–26, 26–27, 29–30, 128; Pauline accounts of, 4; in Qurʾān, 40–61, 61n4, 69–71; in *tafsīr*, 44–54; universality of, 25–26; words for, in Bible, 24. *See also* murder
strangers, 102–3
success, 83–84

*ṭāʿa*, 40–41
*taʿārafū*, 115–16
Ṭabarī, Muḥammad b. Jarīr al-, 62n18, 63n22; reconciliation in, 108–9, 111, 112–13, 114; sin in, 41, 42, 44–48
*tafsīr*, 44–54, 62n18
temptation, 27, 28

Tertullian, 12n19
Theodore of Mopsuestia, 11n7
Thomas Aquinas, 10n3, 32–33, 38n10, 38n14
tolerance, 97–98
traducianism, 11n8, 31–32
Tree of Knowledge, 27, 43, 53. *See also* Adam and Eve; Fall

unity, 136

violence, 9
Volf, Miroslav, 8

Wagner, Samuel, xv
will, freedom of, 4
World Council of Churches, 10

Yūsuf, 59

Zamakhsharī, al-, 56, 114–15

# ABOUT THE EDITORS

**Lucinda Mosher** (ThD, General Theological Seminary) is assistant academic director of the Building Bridges Seminar, an international dialogue of Christian and Muslim scholars founded in 2002 by the Archbishop of Canterbury and now under stewardship of Georgetown University. Concurrently, she is faculty associate in Interfaith Studies at Hartford Seminary, where she teaches courses on chaplaincy, America's religious diversity, and Christian-Muslim relations. With David Marshall, she is coeditor of and contributor to three previous volumes in the Building Bridges Seminar series. She is also the author of *Toward Our Mutual Flourishing: The Episcopal Church, Interreligious Relations, and Theologies of Religious Manyness* and the three-volume series *Faith in the Neighborhood*, plus numerous other book chapters and journal articles. As a consultant, Dr. Mosher takes on diverse projects in the United States and abroad—including service on the Management Group of the Anglican Communion Network of Inter Faith Concerns and ongoing assistance to the Seminary Consortium on Urban Pastoral Education.

**David Marshall** is Jack and Barbara Bovender Associate Professor of Anglican Episcopal Studies and Ministry, associate research professor of Islamic Studies and Christian-Muslim Relations, and director of the Anglican Episcopal House of Studies. A priest in the Church of England and a scholar in the field of Islamic Studies, Marshall holds a PhD in Islamic Studies from Birmingham University. He has served as a parish priest and has taught in a variety of settings, including the universities of Edinburgh, Oxford, and Notre Dame in London as well as in an ecumenical theological school in Kenya. He also served as chaplain to the Archbishop of Canterbury from 2000 to 2005. Before joining the Duke Divinity School faculty in spring 2013, Marshall worked as a research fellow of the Berkley Center for Religion, Peace, & World Affairs at Georgetown University, serving as the academic director of the Archbishop of Canterbury's Building Bridges Seminar for Christian and Muslim scholars. He continues to be involved in this project. He is married with two children.

Lightning Source UK Ltd.
Milton Keynes UK
UKHW012002300820
368968UK00014B/327

9 781626 162846